Stories from the Great War

By Lacey Amy

1916-1918

Stillwoods Edition

Edited by Doug Frizzle

Catalogue Information:

Title: Stories from the Great War
Author: W. Lacey Amy aka 'Luke Allan'
Edited by: Doug Frizzle
Published by: Stillwoods
ISBN Canada: 978-1-988304-21-2
Blog:Stillwoods.Blogspot.Com
Website store: http://www.lulu.com/spotlight/lulubook22

Keywords: nonfiction, world war 1, Eskimo, Shiwak, Lacey Amy

The cover image was suggested from '*The Veteran Magazine*' official organ of the Great War Veteran's Association of Newfoundland.

Chapter	Page

Introduction

W. Lacey Amy, (1877-1962) was a Canadian educated in Ontario before he travelled West to Medicine Hat where he became the editor owner of the *Medicine Hat Times*.

During World War 1, he became a journalist in London, working for a number of newspapers, the *Saturday Night Magazine* and *The Canadian Magazine*.

Here are presented the articles that appeared in the popular monthly, *The Canadian Magazine*, published in Toronto. There were two series 'With Canadians from the Front' in seven parts, and 'England in Arms' in eleven parts.

Also included is 'An Eskimo Patriot', which is his response to the lose of a good friend. The images for this article come from '*Wide World*' magazine.

The blog, **Stillwoods.Blogspot.Com**, contains much more information on the journalist and author. There are also more stories from the First World War.

Thanks to Claudio Murri, who first suggested this series in a 1986 paper on the author.

Doug Frizzle, January 2017.

By Lacey Amy
Part I of 'With Canadians from the Front'
From *The Canadian Magazine*, Toronto, September 1916, No. 5, Vol. XLVII

A Series of articles, of which this, the first, depicts the grim, revengeful determination of the Princess Pats in "That Particular Hell at Hooge."

Map from Wikipedia; originally Canadian War Museum, George Metcalf Archival Collection/drf

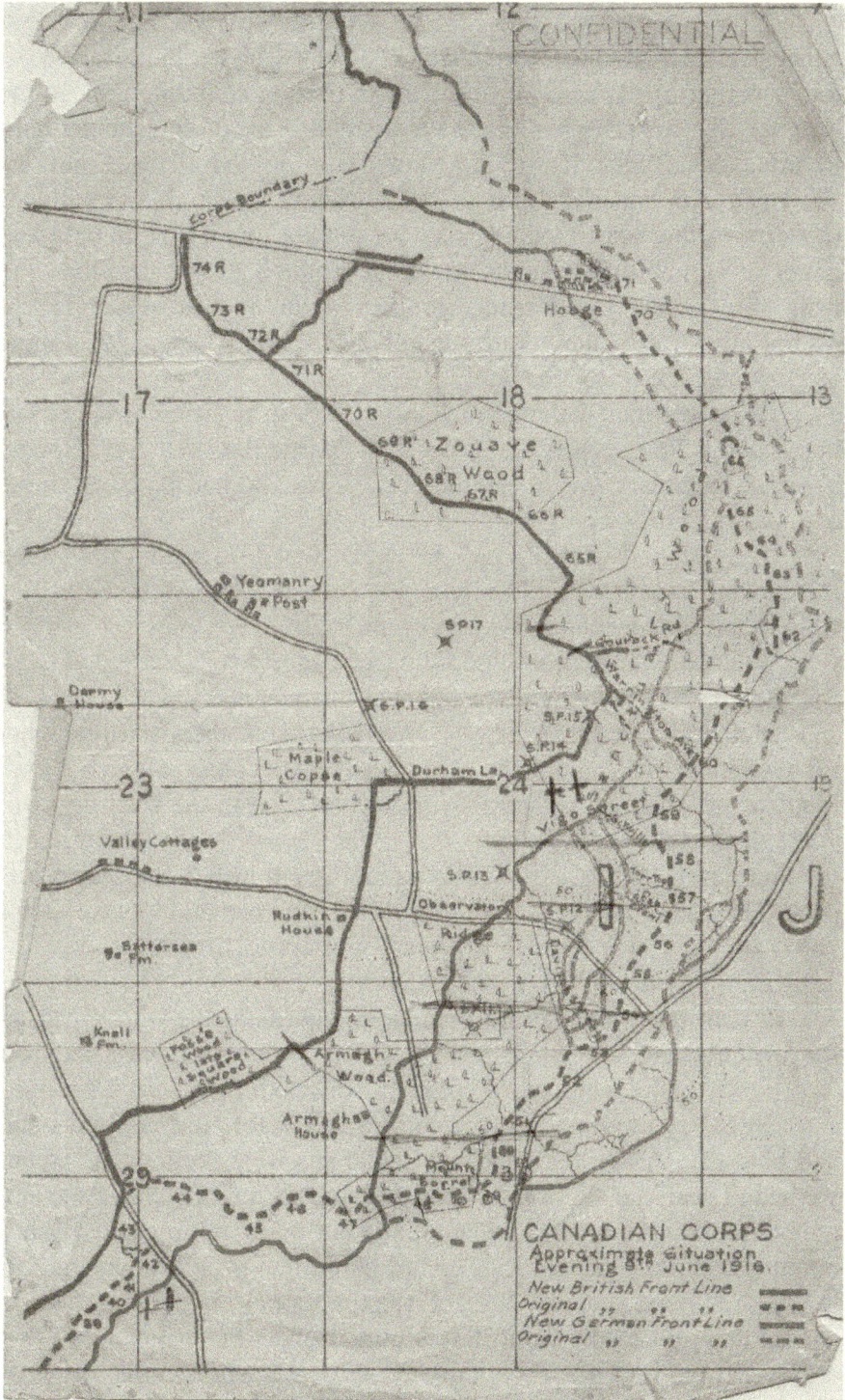

CANADIAN CORPS
Approximate Situation
Evening 3rd June 1916.
New British Front Line
Original " " "
New German Front Line
Original " " "

3

HE was seated on the edge of a white-covered cot, one eye concealed by a bandage, the other, bloodshot and swollen, staring off into a corner of the ceiling. In the stare, in the pendulous foot, in the limp hands lying over his knees was a singular air of detachment hard to understand until it was whispered to me that it was not his bandaged eye that kept him there, but shell shock, that penalty of modern warfare which technicists have not yet found time to befuddle under an unintelligible name. Later he pointed to the neighbouring beds where men lay reading, munching, talking or watching the distant life of the corridors—New Zealanders, Welshmen, Englishmen. He was Canadian.

It was not that being Canadian put him in a different class, but that having just emerged from that "particular hell" at Hooge, between Sanctuary Wood and Zillebeke Lake, he had pictures all his own at which to stare.

"They started shelling us," he said, "that Friday morning, June the second, about nine. The Princess Pats and the Mounted Rifles were in the front trenches, with us on the right."

"You were in the front line?" I asked eagerly.

He looked at me vaguely a moment, then smiled.

"Hell, no! You'll never talk to anyone from the front line—not till Germany gives them up. . . . I saw two come staggering out, blinded, smashed up so bad they would only be in the road up there when the attack came. Only two! . . . The rest are—not talking, or in the German hospitals. I was in a supporting trench a hundred yards back. They let loose on us with everything they had and lots we didn't know anybody ever had, from trench mortars to fifteen-inchers. . . . They didn't let up till two in the afternoon."

I wasn't sure whether he shuddered, but his hands were covering the one good eye.

"Pretty bad, I suppose," I commented weakly.

"Bad! . . . Say, it was a dream of a day before they started—sun and blue sky and all that, and we Canadians were feeling fine again, we hadn't seen the sun for so long. . . . And then. . . . I didn't see any more blue sky. I didn't see anything but trees falling and flashes bursting right into my eyes. . . . and I could feel myself bounce every time a shell burst near me. We got it in the supporting trenches near as bad as they did in the front. I was buried once, but I remember that didn't seem to hurt me, except my eyes. . . . Then at two they came at us over the parapets."

He seemed to have finished, contemplating the picture he had been sharing with me.

"They say the Canadians ran," I spurred him on.

Even one eye can express contempt. "Yes . . . they ran, But—. Back where I was I could see it all, that next fifteen minutes. Yes, they ran. . . . There wasn't a dozen yards of cover in one stretch left of our front trenches when they stopped their big guns. We didn't think there'd be a fellow left to stop them when they came over. But we were wrong. There were a few, most of 'em cut up—but they could run. Fritz came over like sheep, thousands of them. They were dead sure they had it all their own way. And then a few dozen of those boys heaved themselves up from the front line (hosts of 'em tried to, but couldn't) and ran—you're dead right there—bang at Fritz.

"Most of 'em didn't have a thing but a rifle-barrel or an entrenching tool in their hands, but they sailed into that mob of Germans like as if it was a big game or a movie show. . . I remember one big fellow right ahead of me. There wasn't a sign of cover where he got up from—all alone—and he hadn't a blessed thing in his hands. he looked like a scarecrow with his clothes all torn. I watched him. He grabbed a German bayonet and spiff! the German just toppled over. With that rifle he banged about till I couldn't see him for Fritzes. . . . Yes, they ran. I don't wonder the Germans said so. They felt 'em running.

"Then I had other things to do. I was the only one left in my bay and the Germans were coming down the communication trench. One place their shells had filled it in and they had to jump out to get to the next part. I kept my rifle on that place. I thought I'd got them all when suddenly one jumped out in front of me and yelled in English, 'Hands up, friend!' But he was too near the end of my rifle to work that. Then I could see them coming over in bunches, so I dropped my outfit and bolted across to where I heard firing from the Princess Pat trenches. I guess I was pretty well locoed, for I didn't know where I was going. There were dead and wounded all about and one of 'em told me the Pats had retired along their communication trench and I dropped into it and followed.

"About fifty yards back we found a little cover and there we stuck, a mixed bunch from the supporting trenches. They never got us out of that. I think Fritz was afraid we might 'run', too. And they

5

knew we had more than our bare fists. Then a shell came along and buried a few of us, and when I was digging another struck the same spot. I don't know what happened after that."

He pointed up to the end bed of the ward where a soldier lay with closed eyes.

"That's the only other one came out of my bay. He was deaf and dumb at first. He can talk now. Oh, yes, the fellows got him easy enough. You see, Fritz held that supporting trench only about twenty minutes. There was enough of it left to be worth taking. Sergeant—, in Ward—, will tell you how they got it back."

II.

Not one Canadian, of the dozens with whom I have talked, emerged from the Sanctuary Wood fight without showing nerve effects of the terrible bombardment. Some stage of shell shock was visible or in grudging retreat. That in itself is proof of the intensity of the gunfire the Canadians had to endure. Never has there been an engagement where shell shock was such a general result.

In a later article I will have something to say about shell shock, its effect, its treatment and cure. It is the most interesting of the "wounds" of the new type of warfare, and, like the other wounds, is developing a treatment discovered in its entirety only as the war progresses.

One of these shell shock patients, who started even at my appearance in the doorway fifty feet away, was dallying with his supper. A large, piece of headcheese lay on the plate beside his cot, and an orderly was dumping some very appetizing-looking salad and slices of bread and butter inside it. Conversation with him was difficult, for he was recovering but slowly.

He had been on a machine gun battery a hundred yards behind the front line covering a gap. Through the worst of the shelling he lived without a scratch. In his little bit of trench were three Lewis and four Vickers guns the former a machine gun too large to carry. Early in the fight the Lewis guns were buried by the bombardment, and although they unearthed them twice, they were always buried again before they could be brought into use. It was evident the Germans knew they had the range.

Accordingly, with the four Vickers, he and his remaining mates left the trench and hid themselves a few yards further up in a hedge. Their duty was to keep the Germans from rushing the gap in the front lines, and this they succeeded in doing with the Vickers, in spite of the shells that began to search them out. The enemy succeeded in getting into the front trenches, but they did not attempt to come any farther.

All through that afternoon the handful of men and the four machine guns clung to that hedge, spraying the gap, and later the captured trenches. Not until darkness came did they retire to their friends, now rebuilding behind their protection the destroyed trench they had left.

And when the strain was over, the three unwounded gunners broke down. All alone, with the front trenches only a few yards away in the hands of the Germans, with shells showering everywhere, burying them and their guns repeatedly, with hundreds lying wounded and dying all about, with no idea how far the Germans had reached in their rear, they had worked amid a din that drowned the sound of their own guns. No human nerves could stand it. The three were taken back through the darkness to the hospital. What happened to the other two he did not yet know.

III.

Tell the most apathetic shell-shocked Canadian who survives the Sanctuary Wood affair how his mates "ran" and you effect an instant cure, even if it but temporary. Those of the front line who ran must have preferred exposing themselves to the peril the Germans said they were fleeing, to the eyes of their friends. The supporting line did not see them run except forward. Indeed, those who remain from the second line won't admit even a German gain.

They point out that, although the Germans entered the front trenches over a length of three-quarters of a mile, the Canadians got back everything of value within a few hours. In the first overwhelming rush of the Germans following the terrific bombardment, a few of them entered the supporting trenches, but even at that a few of the Pats in one section held on up at the front till morning and then retired when no relief came. In twenty minutes the Germans were scrambling back from the supporting trenches, and had there been enough trench up at the front to take the Pats would never have had to retire.

It didn't take long to convince the Germans that they had taken a larger bite than they could masticate, and when they saw that it was nothing like demoralization they faced from the supporting trenches they turned tail to the mixed band of Canadians that charged up from only fifty yards away. For a couple of hours a few held the intervening bushes and shell-holes, while their friends worked feverishly behind them to bring the old Canadian front line into something like protection, but after that No Man's Land was that hundred yards between what had been the first and supporting trenches of the Canadian line. That the unorganized counter-attack of the Canadians within twenty minutes should have retaken the second line is sufficient comment on the German morale before a "running" enemy.

It was there a member of the 49th took up the tale.

"We had been in reserve perhaps a mile in the rear. We knew there was a big row up in front, but the German curtain fire kept us from moving till night. Then we got up to what had been our former supporting trenches, now our front line. There wasn't a lot of cover even there, but the fellows who'd been in the thick of it were making the most of it and throwing up more. We sent them back, although some over at the side of us hung on for four days before they were relieved. All night long the Germans shelled us in spasms. They sure were nervous that night, and every little while they'd cut loose with artillery enough to have cleaned us out behind that cover if it had been daylight.

"We knew we were down for a counter-attack in broad daylight. When the enemy's expecting you it isn't what you call a picnic. But it wasn't ourselves we were anxious about, but whether we could last out to those front trenches in the face of all those guns. We didn't dare try in the dark, because we didn't know what there was left to take or what we aught to prepare for.

"Well, next morning at eight we got the word. Down the line we could hear them hot at it, and then we got into the thick ourselves. Before started we saw that the Germans had been able to do little towards digging themselves in, but they were there thick, and back of them the machine guns. We got it heavy. Men were falling all about, but we kept on I don't know exactly how far we got but I remember feeling kind of lonely and looking around. There weren't more than fifty of us moving, but a little way back I saw the rest digging in. It didn't seem worth while—fifty of us bucking up against a few million Germans, so we dropped down and crept back."

He chuckled, and snatched from his head excitedly an old knit cap and banged it on the table beside the cot.

"What had happened was we'd gone clean through our old front line with-out knowing it, there was that little of it left, and we were making across for the German trenches.

"We dug in there as best we could but the German guns kept tearing it down as fast as we could got it and that night we went back to the other line and made things solid there. But, you bet, if we couldn't hold it the Germans were in for a time trying to. I got mine late in the afternoon, but managed to crawl out that night when relief came."

The story was rounded off by one of the relieving troops. By that time the Germans were content to leave the new front line in undisputed possession of the Canadians, and the latter were willing to grant the Germans for the time the tragic prize of their former front line on which the Allied artillery was now turned. The new forces sent up made life miserable for the Germans for four days. In the meantime the Canadian wounded had to be treated in the trenches, because the Germans were turning their guns on the stretcher-bearers from the first of the fight.

"Tuesday," said one, "things were quieting down a bit. We couldn't understand why we weren't getting a chance to get back, but it was frightful weather and the Germans were welcome for a while to the beautiful job of holding down that front line till we were good and ready to make it solid when we took it. Then that night they banged at us again, and in the midst of it they set off a big mine close to Sanctuary Wood. I happened to be there. I guess I'm about the only one who got back to a hospital. But they didn't get the hole. The company next us crowded over and sat in that."

One sleeve of his shirt hung loose, but from the outline I judged that his arm was in a sling underneath.

"You'll get your chance," I said, for his eyes were flashing and his left fist was clenched.

His face clouded, and he raised his left arm to his right shoulder. "It's not for me," he said. "I lost this. I'm having another slice taken off in a few days. But, tell me, did they get Hooge back? I know the rest. Here's a letter from a chum who was through it—a lieutenant now."

I couldn't tell him we had Hooge; but in the letter he allowed me to read was the spirit that reconquers the Hooges of life anywhere. It told of the third stage of the fight, of the final sweep of the victorious Canadians.

The battle was divided into three distinct actions. There was the German bombardment and attack, the immediate counter-attack whereby the Canadians won back the old lines, but found them not worth the holding, and the great attack a week later by which the lost trenches were recaptured except in the village of Hooge and reorganized to their former strength.

From the first line trenches very few Canadians have come out to tell the tale. The second stage is told here. The heroes of the third, who swept the Germans before them with a fury that had been bottled for days, are still fighting in France, or were kept there in the hospitals until the big push, now on at the time of writing, was about to commence. No interview can present the picture painted for me in a letter from one of the wounded in the final drive to his friend in an English hospital from the effects of the first few days of the German success. The friend with whom I talked was minus an arm—the one I have just written about. The wounded writer in France had just been made a lieutenant as his share of the rewards for fighting well done. His jubilation, irrepressible by mere physical incapacity, is too contagious not to give in his own words:

"It was hard to think of you fellows going out that way. I know you'd like to have waited here until we got even. And they'd have kept you, I know, until the boys bunged up like you were fitter for travel. But there was not going to be room over here for you when we got going, because when we started after that lost trench there was going to be work for the hospitals here without you fellows choking things. And there is.

"I'm tickled to death you're getting along so well. I knew you would. That's the best of living like you have. My own case doesn't look quite so sure, but I'm not fretting. It would be different if we hadn't done it.

"It was five or six days, I think, after they carted you away that they let us loose at the Huns. We had been stewing to get at them, and I guess our officers knew something had to happen pretty soon. It did not look as if there was trench enough up there to be worth a scrap, but the Germans had it, and it once belonged to us, and that was enough. Well, up there at the top of Sanctuary Wood, where you went up among the tree-tops, we had a whale of a time after they blew that hole. Say, that was some place where we dug in. We were pounded with a terrific shell fire for days. Then they relieved us for a few days—not before it was time—for a lot of us were jumping with the noise and almost deaf, and nearly dead for sleep. And then we went into the same place again, and the assault took place through us.

"I'm sorry, old chap, you didn't last it out so you could have been along. Lord, it was fine. I could feel that terrible fretting of the past week just oozing out as the boys jumped the parapets and smashed across to where our old first line had been. I don't think anything could have stopped them. I didn't get in with the first bunch, because my company was held on the edge watching for the counter-attack, if it came too soon for our fellows to make a stand.

"When we got going we went through the Germans like a knife through cheese. They didn't know what to do with us but throw down their rifles and bolt, or hold up their hands. They said we ran. You should have seen them skedaddle for home and ma, what didn't throw themselves on the ground and beg to be taken. We went clean to the old line and captured some hundreds of prisoners. Our artillery had kept them from doing much in the digging-in line, and so we had a chance to slam them good and plenty. And you bet we did.

"Then we had to take ours. They had the range of us to a nicety, and they gave us particular hell with shell fire for days before and during the assault. When we went up and took over the line from the assaulting troops we had to take another dose of iron, which the Huns put on while they were getting their counterattack ready. But the counter attack never came off—at least, not what we'd call an attack. Our artillery got them in the belt and cut them up too bad to want to come to close steel with us. So we settled down in a day or two as if there hadn't been even a brush, and Fritz was glad to let it go at that.

"During nearly all the last turn-in the rain poured down in torrents off and on, and you can imagine the state the lads were in, with freshly-dug trenches and everything being blown to smithereens by shell fire. Towards the last our trenches consisted of shell holes connected by ditches and carpeted with water and *some* Flanders mud. If a shell burst within a hundred yards we had to get someone to scrape the plaster from our eyes before we knew if we were hurt. You couldn't tell a captain from a Tommy and it didn't matter much just then.

"I'm mighty glad I lasted through it. After they've got me spliced and refurnished it's Canada for mine, I guess. It is if the refitting takes. I'm not so bad just now, and I feel cocky enough to win out. Already I'm short a leg, and goodness know what else I'll need to forage from the factory before they're through with me.

"But we did it, old sport, we did it. We got good and even with them for trying to wipe out the old bunch. Why, the Huns were lying so thick when we drove through that we had to jump them all the way. You and I, old pal, can go back to Canada and join forces and make a whole man between us."

The next article of this series is entitled "The Life-Savers". It gives a graphic and touching description of the work of the stretcher-bearers, the ambulance men and the workers of the Blue Cross.

The Life Savers

By *Lacey Amy*
Part II of the series 'With Canadians at the Front'
From *The Canadian Magazine*, October 1916.—

THE mission of mercy on the battle-field is not the earliest stage of battle, but its importance is not lessened thereby. As the soldier cannot live without food, so a successful campaign does not permit him to die without the best of attention. The men who care for the wounded do not figure in the number of the enemy they kill, but in the number of friends they save. From those daring men who carry relief to the very cannon's mouth, back to the skilled surgeons who give their brains and experience to great war hospitals, the worst of the horrors of war are eliminated by means of an organization that is as complete as the commissariat. The battle is won just as surely by the Red Cross brassard as by rifle and gun.

Through these unselfish, sacrificing men human life in the Great War becomes an individual treasure, not a great mass to be preserved in the aggregate but neglected in the unit. Even to those who understand the tremendous system built up for the soldier's care when he is stricken the fatal casualties are so few as to seem miraculous. Against every engine of destruction the world can devise, against every devilish development of the perverted German mind, the millions of allied soldiers face trench life with as little danger of the final payment as in some of the hazardous occupations of civilian life.

The forces that surround him with a wall of protection that is a constant surprise to him are made up of organization, medical efficiency, and personal bravery. The organization rests in the hands of men who sit at desks far from the sound of the guns, their fingers nevertheless on every beating pulse of the service. Everywhere, from the trenches to the hospitals in England doctors work as they never thought to work, for wages they never expected to accept. But up at the front, where the shrapnel shrieks, where death and disaster lurk in every space, is another branch of the Red Cross that has been unsung too long.

Ask the wounded soldiers who saved their worst suffering, to whom they owe their lives, and the list will be headed by the stretcher-bearers, the fellow-soldiers who brave everything they brave

13

without the satisfaction of taking revenge, who stand and await their call without any of the hysteria of battle or the hope of a safety-valve in some glorious rush. Theirs is the personal bravery branch of the great life-saving service. Beneath the jagged bursts of shell fire, in the face of rifle and machine-gun, where every enemy eye is focused for destruction, the stretcher-bearer, the wounded soldier's friend, crouches at work.

Unarmed, save by the Red Cross brassard on his arm, outfitted only with a water bottle and a medical bag, he clings with his mate close to every bombarded trench, to every hideous crater, to every perilous mission. Where danger is lies his only sphere of duty. Right at the front, or in a small auxiliary trench where he will be out of the way of the fighting men, he awaits the call that is sure to come. There is nothing for him to do to take his mind from the perils, and always his work is with the horrors. Fatigue duty, which is often relief duty, is not permitted him, for he always must be ready. He sleeps fitfully, boots and medical bag on.

It is not even as if he were trained for his work. Somewhere available there is usually one with some medical training, but seldom has the stretcher-bearer time to apply more than what his common sense and growing experience teach him. It is one of the peculiarities of military training that the Red Cross end of war is trained to a finish—in the things that don't matter. Months and months of hard, dry drill are thrown about the careers of thousands of military doctors whose helping hands millions of wounded soldiers are longing for. And never for a moment will those doctors have use for one sentence of what they are driven into before they can apply their skill where it is needed. Many stretcher-bearers enter the front trenches without a knowledge of field dressings, although that is their entire work. But necessity and the very interest they must have in their duties to assume them are swift teachers. For the next war the wasted drilling and time may be eliminated for the training that counts.

"Stretcher-bearers, on the double!" It is the cry the stretcher-bearer is always waiting for. It is always "on the double". Also it is one of the products of the moment of excitement that the report mentions many casualties, even though there be but one. To this excitement he alone dare not yield. Cooly, methodically, he cuts away the clothing from about the wound with a large pair of scissors carried for that purpose, decides instantly as to the necessity of an opiate, and completes the dressing with as little pain as possible.

Always he is in touch with the reserve by telephone. If the casualties are few and slight he and his mate may attend to their conveyance to the dressing-stations at the rear, but usually a fatigue party is sent forward for that purpose. It is seldom that the communication trenches permit the transport of the wounded even on the backs of the bearers. In exceptional cases, however, the wounded are carried "out over" when darkness comes. In the dug-outs or beneath the firing-platform (the raised platform beneath the parapet on which the soldiers stand to fire) they lie through the weary hours of daylight, dependent entirely upon the skill and attention of the stretcher-bearer.

In some battalions there are standing orders that the stretcher-bearers must not go over the parapets save in the wake of an attack. The wounded must be brought in to them by their companions. But with or without orders the stretcher-bearer is everywhere with the wounded, even to the desperate chance of No *Man's* Land, where no sane person ventures unwounded in daylight.

It is these bearers of comfort who bring in the stories of real grit. P. No. 13789, a stretcher-bearer of the 5th Battalion, tells of unflinching heroes who took their wounds almost as a matter of course. One, of the 7th, his right hand gone, the left shattered, lower jaw almost shot away, thirty wounds in his chest and as many in his legs, and two in his abdomen, wrote his name for them on a parados of the trench. Nothing could be done to deaden his pain, for the condition of his jaw prevented his taking a pill, and the stretcher-bearers had lost their hypodermic. But all through the dressings he never winced. His two wrists he held up for the bandages, and as occasion required he shifted his body in order to assist the work.

"Did he get over it?" I asked.

"Pooh!" replied P. "You couldn't kill a fellow like that. He just would not give in."

When heavy "strafing" is on, every wounded man who is able to walk must find his own way back to the dressing-stations. Only the incapacitated are carried out. And the manner in which they respond to the appeal to shift for themselves in order that their less fortunate fellows may be attended to is a record of self-sacrifice and grim grit.

One day when the Germans let loose there was in one trench a casualty list of three hundred and sixty-five. It was impossible even to dress the slighter wounds, and everyone who could had to shift for himself. Of one who had been wounded from foot to chin every stitch of clothing had to be cut, and when they were finished with him the wounded man was swathed like a mummy. It was a terrible moment, with the trench blocked with casualties and an attack impending. The call was given for every wounded soldier who could to make his way back through the communication trenches. One of the first to stagger to his feet was the mummy, a stiff twist on his face, but grit to the last inch of him.

"I should worry," he smiled, took three steps, and dropped dead.

Under excitement men tramp back to the dressing-stations with bullets in their legs, or crawl back with gaping wounds that would, under ordinary conditions, render them utterly helpless. Once when P. and his mate were struggling back over the open with a badly-wounded man, a shell whistled over their heads. P. felt the stretcher suddenly lighten behind him, and then a bounding figure sped past him. The wounded man, startled by the shell, had leaped from the stretcher as a method of progress too slow for the occasion. The last they saw of him he was still racing at top speed. They never learned what became of him.

On another occasion a shell burst in a room adjoining a dressing-station full of stretcher patients. Half the wounded got up and bolted. It was not that they had been "swinging the lead", as the soldiers speak of deception, but that a form of hysteria had put into them unnatural strength.

It is only in special cases that the open is risked for the conveyance of the wounded by daylight. The wounds may be of such a nature as to demand immediate attention beyond the skill of the stretcher-bearer, or one of those strange moments of insane bravado may drive bearer and patient to take the chance. Once a shell claimed two victims in P.'s trench, one with a had gash in his back, the other with wounds they could not fathom and severe nervous shock. It was a case of risking the open or depriving both men of every chance they had. The sergeant looked at P., and P. looked back.

"We'll run 'em out over." said P., whose leave was to start the next day.

"All right," replied the sergeant. "If you're game I am."

It was put up to the wounded men.

"If you can keep still." they told the shell-shock victim, "we'll

16

take you first," The poor fellow realized his condition, but doubted his ability to hold himself under the heavy shelling. After a time he promised to try. But in the midst of the passage, with shells shrieking about them, he could not control himself. Twice he threw himself from the stretcher. Twice they had to stop and force him back.

"If you don't keep still," they warned him, "we'll all be pushing the daisies." But at the next shell his nerves gave way again. Forced to take heroic measures that might seem cruel to the uninitiated, but are sometimes necessary for the safety of the sufferer, they finally reached the dressing-station.

Back in the trenches the other waited. He could not stand to be touched, and they placed the stretcher beside him that he might shift himself onto it. But he could not lie down. All the way through that danger zone they trudged back to the dressing-station, the wounded man resting against P.'s back, a cigarette puffing furiously. And not a shell fell near them. To-day that man is back in the trenches getting even with the Hun with double fury.

At the moment of writing P. is in a convalescent home recovering from shell-shock and slight wounds, the result of being buried by a shell, with many of his patients, fifteen feet beneath the surface.

Sergeant W., of the 13th, has been buried six times, four within twenty-four hours during the big Canadian battle at Hooge in early June. And yet he has returned to the trenches apparently as fit as ever. He was through the terrible crater fighting before Ypres, and every minute of his work for the relief of his wounded companions was under heavy shelling.

While lying in one of the craters recently recovered, dressing the wounded, the Germans blew up the communication trench back to the line. In an adjoining crater a soldier lay groaning with a shattered leg. Sergeant W. crawled over, dressed the wound, and with a companion carried the man through the open back to the protection of the trenches. Not a German fired on them. In this connection it is only fair to say that the stretcher-bearers, as a rule, speak well of the Germans. There have been glaring exceptions, but there is not the deliberate sniping of Red Cross workers we are sometimes led to believe. With but one exception the stretcher-bearers to whom I have talked have expressed their conviction that any seeming inhumanity in this respect has been under the stress of excitement. It must not, too, be taken for granted that even the Canadians are completely blameless. In the strain of action a soldier is scarcely accountable for every bullet he fires.

There are, of course, well authenticated instances of German brutality and callous disregard of the ordinary demands of humanity. I have been told of one instance when an ambulance rushed right across the rear of the front lines in broad daylight, taking on its load of suffering, without a single shot being fired at it. Another time an ambulance had just started back with its burden of wounded, during a lull in the fighting, when the Germans commenced shelling again, obviously of intention, with the ambulance as the mark. Two of the wounded were killed, together with the horses. The rest were hastily unloaded back into the trenches.

The seriousness of Sergeant W.'s work did not prevent his seeing some of the lighter incidents of warfare as coming within the range of the stretcher-bearers. One of his friends had always insisted that, should he be wounded, he would bolt. One day a whizz-bang came over the parapet, into the parados, and a few small fragments slightly wounded him about the head. Instantly he put his hands to his head, shouted the familiar "stretcher-bearers, on the double," and dashed off down the trench. Behind him chased a stretcher-bearer, a Scotsman, pleading in expressive Scots for him to stop, clinging grimly to a pipe and scattering bandages all along the way. W. could follow the course of the chase by the shouts of laughter that came back to him from all along the trench. Right to the section held by the British the fleeing soldier continued, but there he was stopped. Fifteen minutes later Sandy came triumphantly back, leading the bandaged soldier as if he were a German prisoner. He was taking no more chances on that special variety of relief work.

One of Sergeant W.'s experiences was to have a water-bottle shot from his shoulder. With the recklessness that so often comes to the soldier he was returning overland to the trenches through a fog, a bottle of water balanced on his shoulder. Suddenly the sun came out. W. felt a slight jar and heard a crash, and then the water flooded over him. There are cases of rum jars having suffered in the same way, but the lament was always louder.

#

Back of the stretcher-bearers come the ambulance men. At the dressing-stations, and from there back to the hospitals, they complete the work begun by their fellows in the front trenches. Their place is not so dangerous, their work not so arduous in some ways, but they are in closer touch with the more skilled part of the treatment of the wounded. Sometimes, on ambulance duty, they are exposed to shelling, and not infrequently the dressing-stations are under fire.

In the hospitals another body of men continue the care of the wounded. It is with no lack of appreciation of their necessity that the soldier thinks of the R.A.M.C. as the Rob All My Comrades branch. From dressing-station to the hospitals in England the wounded soldier has little chance to pull through with the smallest of the trophies and souvenirs he has so zealously collected in France.

But the hospital workers are not charged with neglect of duty, however free many of them may be with the common pelf of war. His life of grind is lightened with few bright spots, free many of them may be with the Queen's Base Hospital, has been cut short by a physical breakdown from which he is slowly recovering, has seen the active service of the hospital unit in Egypt and France. Formerly an efficient attendant at the Asylum in Kingston, he enlisted with the supply force sent out to the Queen's unit. In Egypt he faced flies and heat and disease. With others he contracted dysentry, was brought to France when the unit was moved to that section of the front, and was given every possible attention in an effort to procure his intelligent service as soon as possible again. Not recovering so fast as they wished, he was shipped to England for the added care possible there. Now he is fighting his way back to health through a nervous collapse. When you feel cold water running off your chest hour after hour it is time to rest up against the strange delusions of war.

\#

B., a well-known Toronto jockey and polo pony trainer, a member of the 58th, enlisted in September, 1915, as one of the comparatively few whose sympathies went out to the suffering horse. A horse to him was more than a dumb, unfeeling creature. Unfortunately he was one of the many who suffered from the red tape and disorganization that is only too evident in some war departments.

He was kept in Shorncliffe for months, not training, but doing odd jobs and acting as batsman to an officer. Reaching France at last, he became ill of pneumonia and rheumatism, and finally reached the hospitals. With the approach of the time when cavalry might again be called into service, he was sent, upon recovery, back to France, where such men as he will be needed.

The development of official recognition of the horse as a combatant factor of war, with all the care of a special branch of the service, is a result of this war, as are a score of other details never before suspected.

The next article of this series will describe the work of the bombers and snipers.

The Bombers and Snipers

By Lacey Amy
Part III of 'With Canadians at the Front'
From *The Canadian Magazine*, XLVIII, No. 1, Nov. 1916.

IT was in the early days of the war when trench warfare was in its experimental stages. Bombing was so imperfectly organized that but forty bombers were attached to each battalion. An order came to bomb out a certain troublesome section of German trench and volunteers were called for. Captain C., a hard-drinking, hard-fighting, reckless, but very popular officer, was given charge of the operation. To the fall-in he addressed himself as follows: "Now, boys, I want twenty of you. I don't want one that's married; I don't want one who doesn't booze; I don't want one who expects to return." It is not an essential part of the story for my purpose that they all volunteered. What is essential is that he wanted only those who would not be missed.

"The Suicide Club" is the soldiers' title for the bombers, and it is succinctly descriptive. There is no more dangerous work at the front. Also there is none more exciting, stimulating, satisfying. As one bomber, lying in hospital with bandaged head and a pair of useless arms and legs, put it with a chuckle: "I tell you the new No. 5 Mills makes the Fritzes squeal; you can hear 'em yelling for miles when we begin."

That is why there is such a rush for the bombing section. The ambition of most of the Canadian soldiers is to get in with the boys who do the destruction out at the front of things; and they practise throwing with an energy that might be supposed to be fitting them rather for the safe jobs in the rear than for the post where anything from a return bomb to a machine bomb may blow them to pieces before they have had the satisfaction of hearing a single German "squeal". The lad with the brass bomb ablaze as an insignia on his cap or tunic is happy and envied by his less fortunate companions.

Bombing is one of the many developments of this war. It is in reality a reversion to mediaeval warfare, with the addition of improvements in bombs and in the manner of handling them. Which includes the additional dangers of these improvements. Starting with but forty bombers to a battalion, the number quickly grew to two hundred and sixty. In each platoon of about fifty-four men eleven are bombers. In addition there is a battalion section of sixty and another lot of brigade bombers. In actual practice there is little distinction between the sections, save that usually the battalion group is kept in reserve.

Since the beginning of the war several varieties of bombs have been tried. The most primitive was the "hair-brush". It was a stick the shape of a hair-brush, about the end of which was tied gun-cotton. With a lighted fuse attached, it was thrown into the enemy's trench. The main trouble with it was that the fuse was of such uncertain duration that it was frequently returned by the Germans to explode in our trenches. Sometimes, indeed, it passed back again; and one of the specialties of the quicker witted was to grab a sputtering "hairbrush" and hurl it back before it exploded, more as a matter of personal safety than for its destructive powers among the enemy.

Another style was struck across the knee before being thrown. It was known as the "Newton Pippen", why I do not know. The main defect in it was that it made a spark when struck over the knee and thereby located the thrower. The "fish-tail" possessed a long stick as a tail to guide its course through the air. It was a concussion bomb, and at best had the virtue of being unreturnable. Then there is the rifle grenade, which is nothing different except in delivery from the other bombs. It, too, was on the end of a stick, which was inserted in the rifle and fired. It has a range of about six hundred yards and explodes upon striking.

But the many types have narrowed down to the No. 5 Mills, a compact, convenient, destructive little affair in shape and size resembling a large goose egg. It is thrown like a baseball, and with all the gusto of a part of a great game. Its principle of operation is simple. Protruding from one end are two small flanges with holes, through which a pin keeps in place a strong spring. To explode, all the bomber has to do is to remove the pin. This releases the spring and in a few seconds the bomb explodes by means of a detonator inside. In many ways it presents its dangers, but its effectiveness and simplicity place it easily at the front. A bomber about to utilize the weapon removes the pin and holds the spring in place with his thumb until it leaves his hand. Fatalities and narrow escapes have occurred by the accidental dropping or imperfect delivery of a bomb from which the pin has been removed, but equal dangers are presented by any of the other types.

The sphere of the bomber is wherever there is an enemy. Day and night, in attack and defence, in surprise raids or general offence, singly or in groups, bombs have been doing work that could be done in no other way. Their effectiveness consists in the thoroughness and wholesale nature of their results. For cleaning out a German trench nothing can take their place, save the artillery, and the limitations of the artillery come where the bomber starts. In attack two bayonet men go ahead to protect the bombers, who immediately follow. After them come the infantry. In crude language, the bayonet men and the bombers are the sacrifice, although, if successful, the bombers may suffer little. In night-work the bomber has the time of his life. Creeping up to the German trenches—through the wire entanglements, if possible—with face blackened to prevent exposure from the flares the Germans use so prodigiously, he hears what he can and then, simply as a token of his visit or for more serious purpose, drops a bomb or two into the trench. Seldom is he troubled by that section throughout his return, for the German who is not disabled is hugging his dugout.

Following up successful attack, the bomb fulfils an equally important purpose. The dugouts that have become such a feature of trench warfare often escape the full blast of the big shells, and within their protection the enemy hides. It has sometimes happened, early in the war before their danger was fully realized, that the Germans thus passed over in a drive have emerged in the rear of the successful attackers and done serious damage, amounting even in one or two cases to the turning of defeat into victory and the capture of the troops that have rushed on to the next trenches.

Later it became the duty of every advancing force to clear out the dug-outs as it advanced. For this purpose there was nothing so quick and complete as the bomb. In the earlier stages of the July drive the more humane method of demanding surrender before bombing the occupied dug-out was general, but when it was found that the Germans took advantage of that either to remain silent or to entice in a few soldiers, whose lives were the sacrifice, the only way was to bomb first and demand surrender afterwards. The German has profited little from his fiendish methods of warfare.

In the work of the Canadians bombs have played perhaps a more important part than anywhere else along the front. At the great battle of Hooge, in June, when the Canadians, driven out of their front lines by the terrific bombardment, made the attack that put them back where they had started from, every man carried two bombs to clear his way, the company bombers eight, and the battalion bombers twenty-four; this in addition to their full equipment. And the wounded who were able kept up the supply of bombs from the rear. The losses of the Germans fully justified this elaborate preparation.

At the crater fighting about St. Eloi bombs were almost the only weapons. In that long-drawn-out struggle for the five craters made by German and Canadian lines nothing else was of much service. Of course, a man showing himself was the target of a hundred rifles, but the struggle was not between visible men. Every crater held its group of indomitable fighters, some German, some Canadian. The artillery was, of course, useless in such cramped quarters, where the combatants were but a few yards from each other through all that bloody stretch of what had once been No Man's Land. It remained to the bombs. From crater to crater these were thrown by both sides. First one side would drive out or kill the defenders of a crater and occupy it, only in turn to be driven out. Those who have been through that awful combat say that it was the most trying experience the Canadians have had. Everyone knew that he was within reach of an enemy bomb that might, and probably would, drop near him, and there was at first no chance of relief. Every inch of exposed ground was covered with machine guns and rifles. Towards the last trenches were gouged out from crater to crater and back to the lines, but largely for the purpose of renewing the supply of bombs. In all crater fighting it is the same, the responsibility of holding the holes resting upon the bombers.

Among the dangerous duties of the bombers is the protection of patrol parties. In these expeditions there are strictest orders not to use a rifle save under supreme necessity. In a pinch bombs are used, not only because they afford a wider protection than a rifle bullet, but because their explosion does not localize too intimately the location of the party. Bombers also protect night wiring parties. During a night raid bombers run along the parapet of the enemy trench delivering their burden of death in the full range of the enemy fire, and down in the trench, in progress from bay to bay, the bomb precedes the advance.

For his work the bomber is equipped with an apron of heavy

canvas, the capacity of which is usually ten bombs. Of course, he carries his rifle, but on his back. He is relieved from all fatigue duty in the trenches.

There are definitely established classes for the training of the bomber, consisting usually of a three weeks' course in England and another week in France. Some of the training has been little better than useless. For instance, at East Sandling a series of lectures, without even the sight of a bomb, was the extent of the training of the bombers, but this was probably one of the weird slips that somehow creep into ordinary military matters.

The Snipers.

Like everything else in this war, the sniper is a distinct creation of the times. And like most else, the Germans led the way until experience taught us the wisdom of their preparations of these many decades. There were months in 1914 and early 1915 when to put but a hand above the parapet meant a half-dozen German bullets in it. In a desultory sort of way the British tried to retaliate. But not until the sniper was made as definite and as organized a unit as the gunner did we begin to establish that superiority that began to be felt about the middle of 1916. In fact, we have never passed the Germans so completely in sniping as in the other details of war.

There are now sixteen snipers to a battalion, under the charge of a sergeant. Their personnel passed from a voluntary system to a careful selection on merit. Men with much rifle practice and reputation were given the chance to demonstrate their ability behind the lines, and if they cared to undertake the peculiar work of the sniper were assigned to duty. Like the stretcher-bearers and bombers, they undergo no fatigue duty, the principal requirements for their business being a steady nerve and confidence. For eight days they are up in the front lines, then a rest for the same time. But they are never allowed to fall out of practice; special ranges are provided for them in the rear.

They usually work in pairs, one as observer, the other as marksman, the duty of the observer being almost as important as his mate's. For the sniper depends as much upon the keen eyes of his observer as upon his own accuracy, since the value of his work and his future safety rest upon his knowledge of the billet of his bullet. The rifle, of course, is fitted with a telescope sight that makes accurate shooting less a matter of light and wind and good fortune than of clearness of eye and steadiness of hand. Marks that would elude the eye as a target are brought within range, and the observer, through his glasses, is able to detect the success of the shot and to correct its error.

When up at the front, snipers are given a free hand. They select their own locations and construct,—or have constructed—their own blinds and protections. Exposed as they are, their safety depends upon the cleverness of their concealment. Sometimes they work in the trenches with the infantry, at which times they operate from an emplacement specially constructed and prepared, no sign of its location being visible to the enemy. Behind the sandbag parapet they make their disposals, with every sort of contrivance to conceal their whereabouts. As many of these have been in successful use every day their description in detail would not be wise at the time of writing; but each sniper develops a few touches of his own to add to the more common ruses. Shooting through tiny spaces in the sandbags, that open and close at the will of the sniper, is the basis of this kind of sniping, the marksman being protected from stray bullets by a steel shield. The back of the hide must be closed in so that the opening of the hole will not be revealed by the sky behind.

But the distinctive work of the sniper is done away from the trenches. Often he selects a spot a couple of hundred yards behind the front lines. There he is far enough distant from the enemy to be protected by the coverings he is able to construct by the means available. He may be lying behind a sandbag parapet of his own, a low, seemingly casual wall that is apt to escape notice in the general chaos of shell-holes and broken trenches. From behind his steel plate, which has a hole in it large enough for the barrel of his rifle and observation, he watches, waiting by the hour, sometimes without results. In more exposed spots he may be protected by a double sheet of steel. But more often his hide is a bit of ruin or a tree. There no rescue is possible should he be discovered, and he is usually open to artillery fire that seeks him out almost as eagerly as the opposing guns. For the sniper is the bane of the ordinary trench-life of the enemy. He may even lie flat on the ground, practically without protection, his face covered with a cloth mask the colour of the surrounding earth or grass, and shoot through a rum jar.

The work of the sniper is not pleasant, either from the danger point of view or from the results. He is not now required to make reports, and seldom will one speak of his successes in detail. One does not like to talk much about the men one has killed in what may savour to some of cold blood; and the officers have recognized that. Some snipers have the greatest contempt for the fellow who will describe the course of his bullet. And yet their work is legitimate and most necessary in the peculiar conditions roused by this war. In attack or counter-attack by the enemy they must pick off the officers. In the ordinary way their duty is more to end the activities of enemy snipers than to disable the rank and file, for the soldier to-day is careful not to expose himself to the sniper's bullet. When the sniper locates an enemy sniper he waits his chance, and the situation of a dozen snipers watching for each other is one to try the nerve of any but the most seasoned campaigner or marksman. If a sniper is especially annoying, the enemy sniper who discovers his whereabout but cannot get him himself directs his artillery to the spot.

He is expected to keep an eye on every enemy movement, a working party, a new parapet, a gun emplacement, and the location of these he passes back to his artillery. Thus a good sniper is a real factor in the war, apart from his less agreeable duties of killing men by deliberate aim. The Germans utilized this branch of the service from the first to an extent that was most difficult to cope with. Not only were their front line snipers well trained and numerous, but their wonderful spy system enabled them to place snipers back through the British and French lines, and hundreds of officers and gunners, whose work is more out of sight of the enemy, lost their lives to them. Any tree or house or ruin was a possible hiding-place, and part of the most serious tasks of the men behind the lines was to keep a watch for this form of menace. As I have said in a previous article, entire gun crews have been cleaned out in this way. One crew had been disabled to its last man without the location of the sniper being discovered. Then a company of soldiers returning to the rear caught a glimpse of a figure in a tree. They did not wait for explanation, for there could be but one.

One of the well-known snipers of the 5th C. M. B. was brought into hospital with shell-shock. From the nature of his duties it might be supposed that his nerves would be above shell-shock, but to be buried far from the trenches, with but one companion and no seeming prospect of escape, is apt to do anything with nerves. By the merest chance he was discovered. He returned to his work, but sniping was beyond him for a time.

He was the ideal man for the job, except physically. Before the war he had been a policeman in an Indian reserve in an eastern province. But he was marked for life with deformities that might have justified him in dropping any work connected with weapons; it was a wonder that he passed inspection for the army. Two fingers of one hand were gone, and an ugly scar across the wrist of the other hand was the mark left by a drunken Indian he was arresting. It had slashed through the cords of four fingers. Yet, from what I could gather of his work, he had proved that a sniper need not be a model of physical perfection. From the first he had been assigned to sniping and had worked with various observers—a couple of big Indians, an Ottawa clerk, who had developed into a grand shot, and a westerner who had the habit of climbing to the parapet to get a better view; he finally paid the bill for his recklessness. J. refused to talk of his successes, but one incident that seemed to have clung to him with a strange vividness was the end of an enemy sniper who was demanding a big toll from the shelter of a tree. After J. had failed for hours to put an end to his sniping he sent word back to the artillery. In a few minutes a "dud"—(a small shell often sent over first to get the range) burst above the tree. Then came a "whizz-bang". That was all. The entire tree disappeared. The calculating deliberateness and calmness of it had burnt itself into J.'s brain for all time.

The next article of this series is entitled "The Weapon of Defence" and will be in the December number. It deals with the changes in fighting methods that have taken place since the great war began.

The Weapon of Offence

By W. Lacey Amy
Part IV of 'With Canadians at the Front'
From *The Canadian Magazine*, December 1916.

AT different stages of the Great War different conclusions have been arrived at concerning the respective values of the various branches of the offensive weapon. Away back when Belgium was standing off the Germans single-handed until the Allies could collect an army, as well as during the following weeks ending at the battle of the Marne, while the British and French were trying to get their breath, there was only one thought in the minds of the experts—guns, guns, and of the largest calibre! Before the great German guns forts previously considered impregnable were reduced to powder. The Allies kept dropping back, crying not so much for men as against the unopposable might of the German artillery.

Then came the turn. The Allies, rallying before Paris, with the Germans puffing from their pursuit and weakened in guns and ammunition by the impetuosity of their advance, stood their ground and fought the enemy to a standstill. The retreat of Mons developed into the victory of the Marne, and trenches began to wind from the sea to the borders of Switzerland. It was then, when Germany stood with her back to her homes, when attack and counter-attack seemed to be deciding between Calais and Berlin, that the critics cooled down and determined that, after all, it amounted to men, not guns.

But when trench warfare seemed to be leading to that stalemate so confidently predicted by German sympathizers and so feared by the Allies a new era dawned. What human waves could not accomplish might be done by a more violent agency. England, Russia, France crowded on steam in the munitions factories and guns began to pour to the front to compete with the German military machine that had been building for three-quarters of a century. At St. Julien it switched from the moment from guns and men to gas. Now and then liquid fire has figured. But for more than a year the swing of the critical pendulum has been once more towards guns; and at guns it promises to stay for the remainder of the war.

There is no chance of the infantry missing its dues. Guns without men to follow up would be no more use towards ending the war than

Zeppelin raids. But men without the guns! That is where Russia stood in June 1915, when her hordes were powerless against the rain of German shells that poured death on them from a safe distance.

Canada has not attempted to maintain her share of the field guns necessary to the support of the number of men she has sent to the front. She has contributed that which she was in a position to give in the quickest time. England, from her greater resources and experience, has added the greater part of the batteries of larger calibre now considered wise for the completion of the force in the field.

Canada has contributed at least three of what are called heavy batteries. Cobourg, Ontario, perhaps the most famous, saw emergency service early in the war. As the only heavy battery available it was hustled about Canada wherever attack from German cruisers threatened. Right across to Victoria it tore in anticipation of the Pacific squadron that never came, and when the danger was over it was recalled to other active duties.

But Canada's heavy batteries, consisting only of 4.7 guns, are light compared with the guns now doing duty behind the lines on both sides. A 4.7 gun, throwing a sixty-pound shell, does a lot of destruction with its "coal-box", but it is when sixteen-inch shells are dropping about that "heaviness" begins to reach the limit. The vast majority of guns are much smaller than either of these. Canada's batteries, and the most convenient size in use by all the armies in the organized batteries, are thirteen-pounders for the horse artillery and eighteen-pounders for the field artillery.

There is as yet in this war no difference in the uses of horse and field artillery, as there is none between the mounted rifles and the infantry. All are doing trench work. And their shells, usually called by the soldiers "whizz-bangs", do perhaps more destruction in the aggregate than all the larger calibres put together. They are exceedingly mobile and that characteristic has saved the day scores of times when the larger guns would have been useless, perhaps even captured.

On many occasions they have proved their worth in emergency to the cost of the Germans. Once—it was at Loos—an eighteen-pounder was rushed right to the front lines. There, at a distance of 175 yards, it was turned on the advancing enemy at point-blank range. Eighty shells it sent tearing into the oncoming ranks; and then the Germans concluded they shouldn't ask too much and retired. When the British lost Messines the Germans began immediately to erect a barricade across the road. Counter-attack after counter-attack had failed and bombing parties had paid the penalty of their bravery. That night a horse artillery gun was rushed up by an armoured motor car. With a few shells the barricade was blown to bits, while the big German shells vainly tried to reply effectively. Right in the middle of the road the gunners stood behind their gun, while the German guns, far back where they could not see, showered the fields on either side, not suspecting that any enemy would dare the easiest location. In thirty minutes the Canadian gun was back in its old place sending over occasional shells at its former range to prevent the Germans enjoying the night. Of course, there were some little wrinkles in the operation which are not for public print, and which have been, and will be, used again as occasion requires.

The placing of the guns is an art in itself. They must be sufficiently near to cover a varied range within the German lines, while far enough back to be safe from sudden raids. Roughly, these smaller guns are placed at 1,500 yards from their target, and at that distance they can search out the front, support and communication trenches with disastrous effect. Their concealment is as necessary as their use, since one well-placed shell from the enemy may clean out the entire crew and disable the gun. In the preparation of their emplacement sandbags figure, as they do everywhere about the front. These bags are built up about the gun, and over them a galvanized roof is built. The roof is covered with sod or clay, according to the nature of the surrounding ground, in order to render it invisible from the air. The sandbags are rubbed with clay or painted green, under similar conditions, that the place may not be discernible from the front. But that is not sufficient. Now that the shelter is complete, no one is permitted to walk behind it, as it would reveal its existence by momentarily hiding him. Usually there is constructed in the rear a hedge, kept green by being rebuilt each day. Only behind that hedge may one pass. There are a hundred such dodges utilized by both sides in the ordinary course of the day's work, and only the most common of these are described. Upon the ingenuity of his concealment depends the gunner's effectiveness and safety.

In connection with every gun is a number of horses, under the care of men who face much of the same danger as the gunners without the satisfaction of getting even. To each gun are six horses and three drivers. In the field artillery the gunners ride on the limbers; in the horse artillery they have horses of their own. As each gun goes into its place for action it is followed by its ammunition wagons, and as required these wagons—almost always by night, of course—replenish the supply of ammunition. In this work there are two stages. From the rear the ammunition column, in comparative safety, carries the ammunition forward to a given point, where it is reloaded into the wagons in direct touch with the guns, and these are taken to the front by the drivers and ammunition carriers. In case of injury to the gunners, the carriers take their places.

While the artillery, owing to its distance behind the front, is not considered as dangerous a sphere of action as the infantry, or its immediate branches, there are times when the gunner is subjected to a shelling which partakes not at all of the desultory nature of front-line shelling. As the aim of every battery is to locate the guns of the enemy, and in this they are aided by an air service that pays little attention to anything else, immediately a gun is located it is shelled into helplessness; and in these days of marksmanship the fate of a discovered gun or battery is unenviable.

Corporal Y., a St. Catharines gunner, a member of the 10th battery of the 3rd brigade, was the victim of another danger to which gunners are exposed. Everywhere through the lines, even far behind the front lines, the Germans have managed to maintain a sniping force that has been of special menace to those whose operations are carried on beyond the reach of the constant rifle firing across No Man's Land. While this menace is decreasing day by day, owing to improved organization and greater care for its extermination, no one is safe. In the comparative retirement of the gun crews these snipers find their most telling opportunity. There have been instances, one to my own knowledge, where an entire crew was wiped out without the discovery of the sniper. Corporal Y., a husky Canadian of six feet, two, received his "blighty" in the foot through this means. Before that he had passed through the usual narrow escapes without a scratch. Once a shell passed right through his gun shelter without exploding. At Wolveringham the battery was shelled out, two shells coming through the officers' mess without doing more damage than the wounding of the major.

Private G., from Sherbrooke, Quebec, a member of the Royal Canadian Horse Artillery, an ammunition carrier and general utility man on account of his knowledge of French and English, is another sample of the powerful Canuck who reached the hospital with a leg injury. When not engaged in carrying ammunition he was back at the rear with the horse artillery as interpreter, a duty assigned to many Canadians from Quebec.

Driver H., Kingston, A Battery, had been at the front a long time without injury, although he had been in the thick of it around Plug Street, where the mud hampered no other branch of the service so much as the artillery drivers. Frequently they were forced to attach ten horses to each limber, and even then stuck. All last winter he was engaged in the delightful task of hauling ammunition right up to the guns through a narrow valley full of shell-holes. Filled with water, these holes froze over, cutting the horses and making the road not only almost impassable, but positively dangerous to horse and man. Floundering in the dark, with shells searching them out, the drivers had to keep the supply up over a road whose unevenness and depths they could never see nor even guess until the horses sank into them.

Ask a soldier what he dreads most at the front, and, after the cold, he will name the trench mortar. These light but powerful weapons are everywhere, dealing out death in terrible doses. Standing right in the front trenches often, they toss hideous projectiles across No Man's Land into the enemy trenches as one would throw a baseball. Time was at the beginning of the war when the trench mortar crew was as unwelcome in a bay (one of the sections into which the trenches are divided) as a fifteen, inch shell. From bay to bay the trench mortar was cursed, and only when it arrived where the N.C.O. in charge had not the strength to insist upon its removal was it allowed to get in its work. For a mortar was certain to draw a heavy bombardment from the enemy. Now, with the organization of trench warfare, this has changed. The mortar is placed under orders, and no local objections have weight. Which does not modify the local cursing.

The trench mortar is portable. Therein lies its efficiency. It is built on a base that is covered with sand-bags to hold it firm while it throws its bombs over at the enemy. The old mortar threw a sixty-pound shell that had a range of 280 yards. From that the size grew to 192-pounds, throwing across 800 yards and making a hole twenty-eight feet deep, it is said, and twenty-six feet square. It was a miniature earthquake when it struck, and it was little wonder its presence brought the attention of the enemy artillery of all sizes. The latest development is a small affair, called the Stokes gun, weighing but fifty-two pounds complete, and presenting the enemy with an eleven-pound high-explosive. The war is passing more and more to high explosives.

The Stokes gun looks like a bit of stovepipe, and is most useful for sniper's plates and gun emplacements. One of its advantages is that it is even more silent and unseen than the other mortars, all of which emit little noise, and only a few sparks at night. Its thirty-two shots a minute are sure destruction to a wide section of trench. The secret of the new mortar was long zealously guarded. There were standing orders to destroy it at any cost before capture, one shell being carried solely for this purpose. It is reported that the Australians failed, losing two to the enemy.

The projectile of the trench mortar is more a bomb than a shell, with a tail to guide it, bursting either by time fuse or concussion. In the latest designs the shell carries its own charge for propulsion. The Germans, early in the war, had this style of warfare much their own way, but, as in everything else, the Allies caught up. The aerial torpedo of the Germans was for a long time the special terror of our soldiers. Passing very high, it dropped square into our trenches and did much destruction. For a long time there was a special reward of six months' leave and £50 offered to the soldier who would bring one in unexploded. The nearest to success was a British soldier, who loaded one on a transport—and himself, horses and wagon paid the penalty. Of late the Allies have ceased to worry about it since they have something more effective. The ordinary bomb from the trench mortar is clearly visible through the air in the daytime. It is at night that its silent "puff", in disproportion to its execution, is most dreaded.

Private P., Montreal, of the 2nd Division trench mortars, is one of but seventeen remaining of the original 142. His appearance in the casualty list was due to losing his way and thereby coming under the shellfire of the enemy. With fifteen others he was carrying up ammunition by night to a new trench mortar position. Each with his sixty-pound shell, led by a corporal, who alone knew the location of the gun, they found themselves in the German trenches. On their way back they were discovered by a listening post. A shell dropped among them and twelve of the sixteen were killed. P. managed to crawl away, but another shell buried him. While not seriously injured, the not unusual shellshock following burial resulted.

If the Germans have taught us one thing more than another it is that machine guns can take the place of armies in many of the operations. We were slow to realize this fact, as we have been slow to show our willingness to learn many of the other valuable things so apparent from the first of the war. Now we are catching up even in this branch of offensive service. Without machine guns, even with the most powerful artillery, it is doubtful if an attacking force of determined nature could be stopped. The usefulness of the artillery stops a hundred yards or more in front of one's own lines. Rifle fire, while necessary and deadly, is inadequate. A dozen riflemen and a machine gun are almost as effective as one hundred rifle-armed men. It was a knowledge of this that enabled the Germans to make such serious opposition to the Allied advance in July. It is said that there have long been sections of the German front manned by entirely inadequate numbers, but made efficient by machine guns, a product of factories not affected by the "policy of attrition" so confidently adopted by the Allies for the first two years of the war.

The fact that Canada's eager contribution of funds for machine guns did not develop into what was hoped for, is no proof that the guns were not needed. While not of much service for active attack, they are indispensable for stopping the counter-attacks whereby we hoped to make the enemy suffer even more than by our artillery. There is no doubt that the rifle of the future will be a miniature machine gun.

The Canadians have been armed with three kinds of machine guns, the Colt, the Vickers, and the Lewis. The former, an American gun, has been almost superseded by the Vickers, an English production, and at the time of writing a still newer style is under test and the new machine gunners are being trained to its use.

The Vickers is a large gun, requiring an emplacement, and while portable, is beyond the strength of one man. It is now built with a tripod, which facilitates its use under conditions impossible to the old style. It is a powerful gun, firing from belts at the rate of about 500 a minute. Machine guns of this nature are fired from prepared positions. While often brought right into the front trenches, they are usually operated from a support trench or from an emplacement some yards in the rear. As in the case of artillery, concealment is an absolute essential.

When used in the front lines, an emplacement is built up so that the gun is above the level, and the parapet is left before it as before the rest of the trench. When operated from the rear, a more elaborate shelter is constructed. The general design of the shelter is a trench-like excavation on three sides of a square. On the higher centre the gun is placed, and in the trench, so that they are able to work the gun with ease and be partly protected, the gunners stand. In front sandbags are heaped, finished off to resemble the surrounding ground, and overhead, as a protection from the prying eyes of the aeroplanes, a roof covered with grass or mud is erected.

Except under attack, machine guns are operated only by night. The location of one of them meets instantly with a severe shelling, or when in the front lines, with the German aerial torpedoes. In the daytime the gun is entirely concealed and silent, but the crew may be engaged in obtaining their sights for the night work. It may be a sniper's shelter or an emplacement, or a bit of new work that is to be destroyed. When darkness comes the concealing sandbags are re-moved and the gun is fired through a bag of grass to hide the flash. In the use of the machine gun the range is sometimes almost as important as with the artillery. For its ordinary night operations of destroying work observed in the daytime, its aim must be accurate. Frequently an emergency calls for the temporary use of the gun elsewhere. In order that this might not nullify the range secured, perhaps with much daring, the gunners have invented various range-keeping devices that enable them to pick up the range again upon their return. A box, a sheet of paper with a hole in it, and a candle form one of the simplest and surest of these devices.

One of the most effective uses of the machine gun is the night firing in the direction of a suspected exposed foe. Thousands of the Canadians have been caught by this blind firing. By some noise, or by a flare, a patrol or wiring party is suspected. Instantly a machine gun is turned in the general direction, and the sweep of bullets turned loose over the whole area. Only by lying down is there escape, for a machine gun turned slowly will cover the ground so closely that scarcely a fly could escape on the proper level.

Machine Gunner B., Toronto, one of the 1st Canadian Motor Machine Gun Company, outfitted, I think, by Clifford Sifton, has experienced the lot of the men recruited for a service not adapted to the present style of warfare. Like the cavalry and the mounted rifles, they were forced to get down and fight in the trenches like the infantrymen. The machine guns were removed from the cars and taken into the trenches, but the cars found sufficient service in other ways to make them valuable. The machine gunners' turn in the front is much longer than that of the other soldiers. Sometimes they are on duty sixteen days, with seven days' rest. It is not implied that their work is any harder on that account, for the duration of duty has been graded as nearly as possible to the work and exposure and danger endured. B.'s "wound" was shellshock, his convalescence being delayed by an attack of gastritis. His fourteen months in the trenches earned him the rest in the hospitals.

STOKES TRENCH MORTAR, 3-INCH, MARK I,
FITTED WITH TUBULAR MOUNTING, MARK II.

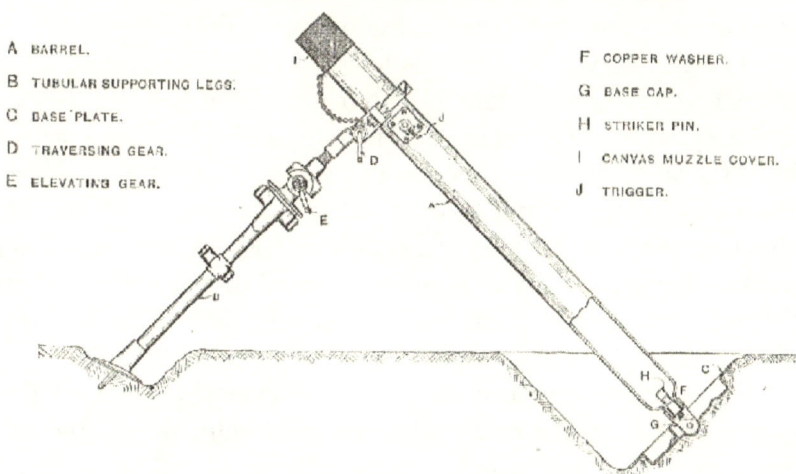

A BARREL.

B TUBULAR SUPPORTING LEGS.

C BASE PLATE.

D TRAVERSING GEAR.

E ELEVATING GEAR.

F COPPER WASHER.

G BASE CAP.

H STRIKER PIN.

I CANVAS MUZZLE COVER.

J TRIGGER.

War Infirmities and Therapeutic Marvels

By W. Lacey Amy
Part V of 'With Canadians from the Front'
From *The Canadian Magazine*, January 1917.

In a study of the war it is uncertain which rouses the most wonder, the engines of destruction, the unprecedented physical effects on the soldiers, or the development of surgery and medicine. The remarkable advance of the destructive machine I have already treated in part, although each succeeding week proves that there is no limit to it. At the time of the penning of that part there were no "tanks", although a few of us had some unproclaimed idea of their coming; and even they are but the beginning of war's frightfulness.

The side of war less known to the public, because less dramatic, less pleasant to contemplate, less immediately material to the progress of victory, is the physical conditions induced by this novel struggle. In the old days of stand-up fighting, of mere guns and rifles, where some shadow of honour clung to both sides, there was small incentive to advanced surgical methods and practically none to new medical ideas. Soldiers fell pierced by a bullet or a sword or a lance, and the result differed immaterially from the accidents of daily life. Sickness was merely the sickness of civilian life and was treated as such.

But with the arrival of trench warfare everything altered, from the training of the soldier to his ailments and treatment. It is no longer a matter of passing out from a camp to a pre-arranged battlefield, like a great military tournament, with retirement at fall of darkness for rest and care of the wounded. There are no camps now, save rest-camps, where the soldiers are out of the struggle for a definite period. The fight is carried on without ceasing from exposed trenches that make camp life at the rear a rest indeed. And retirement is temporary defeat; rest is but the substitution of brigades or divisions whose period of relief has expired.

Whoever heard of "trench-shins" or "trench-feet" before this war? Or of shell-shock? And even nephritis and rheumatism and hernia, while illnesses of peace, have become much more the illnesses of the style of warfare in Flanders and France. "Trench-shins" may sound like a flippant name for an unimportant ailment, but to the sufferer it is temporarily as bad as a serious wound and less eager to respond to treatment. In reality it is a form of rheumatism that attacks the lower part of the leg in painful form, due to standing in mud and water. It is as incapacitating in time as a shrapnel wound. "Shell-shock" is more descriptive, but fails utterly in the indefiniteness of its application; for shell-shock may range from a mere mental surrender of the moment to staring madness or complete and everlasting paralysis.

Nephritis, an inflammation of the kidneys, has attacked many an otherwise strong soldier, and at the first of the war was not appreciated in all its seriousness by the doctors, largely because its inducement by such a condition was, of course, entirely new. But soon it entered into the list of diseases which received special consideration and yielded to modern therapeutics with gratifying readiness. Of course, in its favour stood the physical record of the sufferer, whose presence in the army denoted a constitution prepared for its eradication. That it was taken in time stands to the well-being of hundreds of Canadians whose previous health had unfitted them for describing their symptoms to the doctors.

Other kidney diseases have been induced by exposure in the trenches, being assisted by conditions of diet and bodily protection and care. But with the more careful study of results the soldier has been safe-guarded in a manner never thought possible at the beginning of the war.

The menace of rheumatism was more thoroughly understood from the first, and it has always received special treatment. "Frozen" feet are seldom frost-bitten, but a form of rheumatism caused by the continued cold and damp. The provision of trench mats, a raised slat walk along the bottom of the trench, has done much to keep feet dry—at least to give them a chance to dry. Never after that awful first winter have those fathomless depths of mud so inconvenienced and threatened the soldiers.

Although I have never heard hernia officially recognized as a war injury, I have come across too many cases not to see the connection. In modern warfare the manual labour forced on the soldier is infinitely greater than at any other stage of war's history. Always there stands within easy range of rifle fire a great line of men who must be kept supplied. There are trenches to dig at fever pace and under all kinds of conditions. There are wire fences to erect, wounded to be retrieved under fire, strenuous night patrolling. And, while motor transport has been developed to completeness at the rear, everything near the front line is the work of human hands.

Take an ordinary night's duties. A relieving column is going in. That in itself is a novelty of this war. And each man carries a load that would frighten him under peace conditions. In addition to his equipment of rifle, cartridges and pack, he probably staggers along under a roll of barb wire, or fence-posts, or extra supplies for those who remain at the front. And the conditions of approach to the front line are in themselves a strain. Perhaps for miles the incoming soldiers twist and turn and bump along through utter darkness in a trench not wide enough to give them ease of swing, and so crooked that a wall always seems to be facing them. Here and there are holes, probably filled with water, cave-ins, the chaos of recent shelling, dropped equipment and supplies. The physical strain is, of course, tremendous. And to evade the irritation of blind trench progress some who prefer to risk the open stagger into shell-holes or deep trenches whose first announcement is coincident with a few broken ribs or a bruised body. Walking unannounced into a six-foot trench in the dark is not a recreation to encourage.

The most interesting of the physical effects is shell-shock, both from the variety of its evidences and from its treatment. Essentially a thing of this war, its every mood and twist is a novelty which has called to its study the best medical minds in the country. While in every case shell-shock is a nervous affection, it is far more varied in its forms than anyone but those in daily touch with it would suspect. There are those who maintain that fifty per cent. of the soldiers, even including those in the trenches, suffer to some slight extent from it; and my own observation leads me to believe it. Its existence is noticeable in a petulance at unnecessary or sudden noise, and in the apparently unreconcilable effects of extreme sensitiveness to irritation and extreme indifference.

In its least serious recognized form it may go no further than a slight trembling under excitement, perhaps a profuse perspiration. Sufferers by the thousands have been temporarily relieved of trench life for nothing more than a startled shrinking at the sound of a gun. It has been found that it is much better to give the sufferer a chance to recover from the first slight symptoms than to leave it until months of careful treatment is required. A slightly more advanced stage in some is the perspiration that breaks out, the debilitating effects of which anyone can appreciate.

Of course, shell-shock is the result of the guns. In some cases it may come from the mere overwhelming roar itself, as anyone may have felt the mental irritation caused by the uproar in a stamping mill. But usually the physical condition of the soldier protects him until the shells begin to crowd him in quantities that leave him no time for recovering his poise. But the event of bombardment that claims its shell-shock victims by the score all along a much strafed line is being buried by the earth thrown up by an exploding shell. Very few cases of shell-shock have I encountered that were not induced by this terrifying experience or started on their way by it.

The story of shell-shock lends itself to dramatic effects, to startling narration of incident, for in it lies at times the weirdness of mental unbalance, of physical uncontrol, of ludicrous action, of mystifying and sudden recovery.

Where the effect is slight—it may not appear slight to the uninitiated—the sufferer usually treats it so lightly that the onlooker sees but the funny side of it. This is increased by the knowledge that shell-shock is ordinarily but temporary in its serious effects. For instance, seated at a card-table one evening with a French-Canadian soldier who looked fit for any trench, someone brushed a tiny ashtray into his lap. Instantly, trivial as the incident was, one hand began to shake so violently as to threaten the table itself. It was early in my acquaintance with shell-shock, and while I recognized it immediately I was much embarrassed for the sufferer. But embarrassment was uncalled for. For a second or two he watched his own right hand waving back and forward as if it belonged to someone else. Then he calmly seized it with his left and held it still, smiled down on it, and addressed it in the most pleasantly detached manner: "Hold on, there. Easy now, easy." Twenty seconds later he was dealing.

The relieving feature of it is that the boys themselves treat it so lightly. A certain few make fun of it in others, and lay it to "funk". But there is none of that in the vast majority of cases, V.C.'s suffering with others, colonels with privates; and many of them are as eager as their more fortunate comrades to return to the fight. While, of course, it is "nerves", it is a form that comes so suddenly in its worst type as to be uncombattable. To me it is always distressing, and sometimes beyond description in its dire effects on the nervous system for the time being.

One of its worst forms is to deprive the sufferer temporarily of sight, or speech, or power of movement. That mental equipment has some influence on it seems evident from the fact that, at least in these forms, it is much more prevalent among Imperial than among Canadian troops. One Canadian soldier I know was paralyzed at first from head to foot. When I met him power had returned as far down as his legs, and he was most cheerful and hopeful. Slowly life crept downward, accompanied by pains like rheumatism, and soon he was walking.

The cures—that is the wonderful part of it. Being "nerves", it sometimes demands treatment that might appeal to the outsider as cruel. There are in London special hospitals devoted to its cure. It was found that the treatment it demanded could not be administered in the ordinary hospital, nor could the disease be studied save by those whose attention was undiverted by the other injuries of war.

The essence of treating mere trembling is absolute mental rest, with sufficient physical exertion to keep the mind engaged without fatiguing body or mind. This, too, is the method for the final stage of recovery in all cases. By the experiences of one convalescent home situated in the midst of a large garden, work in the garden produced surprising results. The patients were set to raking or tending flowers or keeping a certain path in condition. On the results was founded a special hospital at Buxton. The work must be quiet, free from sudden noises and movements, and restful in every way.

The treatment for the various forms of paralysis is different. The very principle of it is surprise. Which should prove the diversity of shellshock. A man whose tongue refuses to express itself, whose eyes refuse to register, whose limbs refuse to perform their work, must be taken out of himself. The recoveries are usually amusing. A dumb man by mistake presses to his lips the lighted end of a cigarette—and cusses involuntarily. A friend tries to cheat him at cards—and in the blaze of the moment is told the particular kind of rogue he is. He falls into the water—and screams for help. One dreamed that he was entangled in the German wire and shouted his fear.

Blindness is more difficult because it cuts off the most active sense and makes counter-shock less startling. But it yields like speechlessness in the end. Paralysis forgets itself. One shell-shock patient rose from his invalid's chair and leaped into the Thames to save a sinking girl. At a "revue" an actor fired a pistol, and a helpless paralytic jumped to his feet.

It is the knowledge of these recoveries that has developed a treatment, along lines hitherto unrecognized by therapeutics. In shell-shock hospitals mesmerism is a standard experiment that is frequently effective. The doctors bully unmercifully at times, until the exasperated dumb patient expresses his anger. More than one has found it impossible except by word of mouth to convey his repugnance at the doctor's frank conviction that he is faking. A doctor comes to the chair of a paralytic and suddenly orders him to stand. In sheer surprise and alarm the patient may obey. Or the doctor seats himself quietly by the bedside of a speechless patient asleep and begins to talk. The patient awakes and replies before he remembers his affliction. Once a nurse so angered a patient by telling him that he was no gentleman that he exploded in a vivid recital of his impressions of her, although he had not spoken for weeks.

In another case speech returned to the soldier through embarrassment. The nurse accompanied him to a barber's, excused herself while he was in the chair, and when settling time came the poor soldier found he had not a cent. He began to explain that he would return with the money.

Again, friends of the sufferer lay themselves out to cure him. An Australian was made to speak by his friends cutting the cord of a hammock in which he lay above a stream. As he clambered up the bank, boiling with rage, "Who the—did that?" he roared. Trick cigarettes and matches are given, to explode near the patient's face. Bent pins are placed beneath them. Bad news is suddenly delivered. They are cuffed and booted and trodden upon and generally made miserable. And sooner or later some instinct within protests at further maltreatment and yields. The dumb or blind or paralyzed shell-shocked soldier leads the life of a dog—for his own good.

For the ordinary cases, especially where the evidence of shell-shock is localized in a limb, massage is most beneficial, the subtle progress of the treatment from soothing gentleness to stiff kneading and rapping—always under medical advice—breaking down the barrier of nerves.

Perhaps the disease which the public and the soldier have most feared is spinal meningitis. Evidence seems to prove that the Canadians brought it to England early in the war, but its spread—in so far as it did spread—cannot be ascribed to the Canadians. The infection of an English nurse who died from it was traced to her association with a Canadian officer, who was found to be a germ carrier; but other cases have developed in France where there were no Canadians.

There has not been much loss of life from it, and its treatment has advanced to the point where there is little danger. I have talked with a number of Canadians who have completely recovered, although recovery is slow. It seems that the disease is being carefully watched, and when taken early is not necessarily dangerous. Three or four English physicians have made a special study of it.

At this time it is safe to say that at one stage of the war the most serious menace to the English arms was measles. The details of its prevalence during two or three months of the second year will probably never be known, but whole camps were in quarantine. No one but the authorities will ever know the anxiety that prevailed.

In the surgical department has been the most remarkable advance. It was quickly found that the greatest danger was not from the wounds themselves, but from a variety of sepsis that seemed to breed in the very soil of France. Wounds in themselves trivial developed seriously, and the word went forth that the utmost endeavour must be made to dress the slightest wounds as quickly as possible and to get the wounded man back to the hospitals without delay. There the main effort was towards frustrating septicaemia. Success has been marvellous. Even shrapnel wounds, the worst of all and the most likely to become infected, are looked upon with less anxiety.

The very method of disinfecting altered, and as this is writing it is still altering. That, of course, is the essence of wound treatment. The old application of peroxide of hydrogen, the standard the world over before the war, has been left somewhat in the limbo of the past. Iodine, in various forms, is the immediate hope; and it has justified itself. In hospital it changes again. A simple saline solution that anyone can make in a few minutes is the universal disinfectant and cleanser. Its curative properties have astounded the profession. It is a return to grandmother's remedy, but slightly altered in preparation and strength.

Now a newer method is being experimented with by the celebrated America physician Dr. Carrol. His solution is simple but more or less arbitrary at this stage, and its application is a development of flushing that has prevailed for many months at the front. The result thus far is a wound healed in a fifth of the time formerly considered satisfactory.

There are, too, several discoveries that assist materially in the healing process. For instance, an English doctor has experimented successfully with the application of a celluloid covering to the wound beneath the dressing. The celluloid does not adhere, and in redressing the wound is never irritated and the patient is saved much suffering.

Much of the success of the hospitals depends upon the attitude of the wounded. Never have men gone through so much with such lightness of heart, such unfaltering courage. I will never forget a visit to one of the largest London hospitals where special attention was paid to face wounds. The doctor, showing me some of the worst cases—I would soon have had enough had it not been for the cheer of the sufferers—brought me to a bed where a Scots lad had received enough shrapnel in the face to have killed him at any other stage of the world's medical development. I will not describe his face, as it had healed. Sufficient to say that one eye was gone, the other equally useless for any practical purpose.

"How the things to-day?" inquired the doctor, in that careless way which alone admits inquiry concerning health. In the broadest of Scots the poor, deformed face lifted itself towards the doctor's and a patient smile twisted it. "Canny, doctor, canny." Then with a surge of exultation, as if every ill had dropped from him: "I can see the light."

"I can see the light!" How petty the indispositions of civilian life!

"What got you?" I asked a Toronto lad, the terrible condition of whose head was concealed by dressings that had been changed twice a day for a year. He grinned. "Don't know. Must have been a sixteen-inch shell, direct hit, I think," he laughed. His only worry was how the silver plate which he would be compelled to wear through life would act under the cold of Canada.

The work of the surgeons is beyond belief unless one is moving amidst it. Thousands of men will return to Canada capable of resuming their work, who would never have had a chance under the surgical knowledge of even the beginning of the war. And thousands whose lives would have been unbearable will suffer only slight inconvenience. The small proportion of deaths would have startled even the theorists of pre-war days. And so much of the recovery is practically painless that the wounded soldier is openly congratulated by his companions. It means "blighty" for him, and comparative comfort.

"You shouldn't be here; you should be dead," blurted out a doctor to a lad whose forehead, from temple to temple, a bullet had ploughed. And the fortunate fellow knew no inconvenience save the dressings.

Hospital is pretty nearly heaven to the soldier who has spent much time in the front lines in the winter season. I personally know many of them who, convalescing in the summertime from old wounds, purposely deceived the doctors so as to return to the trenches by early fall with the chance of getting back wounded to the hospitals for the winter. It is one of the best influences on his fighting that a soldier dreads the trenches more than the wounds that will send him to the rear. He may be killed—although the chances are unbelievably small—but if he is only wounded he is willing to take the chances.

The last stage of refitting the soldier for the fight of life is worth a book to itself. New limbs that act almost like the original, nerves and bones that are made once more to do their work, muscles that are renewed—the details are as wonderful as the rareness of amputation. And still medical science is in its infancy. That is one of the grandest results of the war, that the science of human conservation recognizes more than it ever did its incompleteness and is determined to seek the remedy.

War is indeed terrible, but much of its terror has been eliminated by the call of necessity. As the engine of destruction amplifies, the problem of conservation and physical salvation grows with it and goes even beyond it.

133

THE
CANADIAN
MAGAZINE

PRICE 25 CENTS

1 9 1 7

FEBRUARY

The New Governor-General
By Hugh S. Eayrs

Our Strangle-Hold on the German
Spy System
By William Le Queux

Abel and His Great Adventure
By the Author of "Anne of Green Gables"

The Minister of Finance
A Sketch of Sir Thomas White
By William Lawson Grant

THE ONTARIO PUBLISHING CO. LIMITED
TORONTO

The Listening-Post and the Despatch-Bearer.

Part V of 'With Canadians from the Front'
By W. Lacey Amy
From *The Canadian Magazine*, February 1917.

HE was a woeful looking figure when I saw him first—thin, sickly, stoop-shouldered, with a light growth of fair hair in constant rebellion. His white, wan face carried a story I longed to hear. As the kind treatment of the convalescent home began to have its effect, he brightened to its influence, his cheeks began to fill, his colour to return, and the misery in his eyes passed into a deceiving innocence that covered depths of mischief. But always the mere mention of his life in the trenches drove him back to sober thoughtfulness.

He never should have been there at all. Only the sheer grit of him had kept him from the hospital many a time. And when he left us once more for the front there was grit in his last smile. He had not learned to look forward to the bully beef and mud with any greater pleasure; but he knew what was expected of him, and his friends—the very friends who had always taken advantage of his mild ways—would tell you that he had never been found wanting in that.

A Canadian to the tips, he was not born in Canada. Indeed, even when I knew him, he spoke English imperfectly. He was born in France. Perhaps that accounted in part for his willingness to face the fight again as soon as the doctors thought he could, when many a bigger, better lad was adding a touch of limp or cough or a twist of pain when the examining doctor came.

From what level of French society he came is immaterial. His father died when he was very young, and his step-father was cruel to him. At thirteen he ran away. He had heard of Canada even at that age, and it sounded good to him. But the French boats would not take him without his parents' consent; so he shipped on a Norwegian.

His story of the trip across is a series of brutality worthy of the Germans. His mild manners, I suppose it was, and his immature age made him a butt for the cruel sailors. He was kicked and cuffed. A favourite pastime of the crew was to force him to climb the mast when it was caked with frozen spray; and at every slip they kicked him up again. And then he came to Canada, undergrown, ill-nourished, his constitution undermined.

Landing first in the Maritime Provinces, without a word of English at his command, he nevertheless found work. From job to job he drifted into the lumber woods. And there he was, where the harshest conditions of life demand the strongest, hardiest frames, when the war broke out.

One would think that such a career would have hardened him to anything the trenches had to offer. Lads from homes of luxury had stood it, most of them with less grumble than comes from those who had always existed beneath the knocks of life. But the little French lad's constitution had been weakened when he was too young to profit physically from the buffets of his experience. The new kind of exposure told on him from the first. He did not drink, and some of his mates have told me what a pitiful sight he was in the cold, wet dawn, shiveringly refusing his grog, while everyone else was clamouring for the touch of liquid fire that opened each day through the cold season.

But to a man they repudiated the thought that the boy was any the worse for it in the long run, certainly not in morale. "Whenever there was any particularly dirty job on, V. was the first to volunteer," they said. "He never funked. He was on listening-post longer and oftener than anyone else in the company. Grit clear through!" And his illness came to him when his perils seemed to be over for the time. "I thought I was going to Heaven," he breathed to me, in that sentimental way of his, "when I got my first leave." He nearly did. In England but a day or two, he developed pneumonia—as many another has done. That was how I met him.

Always back in his eyes was a sadness, as of looking at pictures he did not like to talk about. But when he did talk I could see a little of what he felt; he described it to me with the simple clarity of a mind that does not make a habit of speaking all it thinks.

It was his listening-post duties of which he was always thinking—those lonesome, terrible, perilous hours of which he had spent more than his share out before the front lines. "Often I used to wish a bomb would fall beside me," he confided, "and get me out of it. But they never would. Fellows all about me were killed, boys who didn't want to die, but I always escaped. From November when I went in I was never dry. Two or three times I found dry places to sleep, and it was wonderful." And never a hint that his duties had been volunteered, that he had offered to go out and lie in the mud before the German trenches while his comrades held back.

V.'s battalion had a particularly bad spot in the line. The trenches were shallow; to go deeper was but to wallow in deeper water. The German line was out across a brutal No Man's Land where water lay in every depression. Men were drowned there. The trenches were bad; the listening-post was inhuman. And the shivering lad returning from before the German fire had no warm dugout to look forward to. He was never dry.

Listening-post duty is the local spying system of the front lines. Every night No Man's Land is inhabited by two parties, the patrol squads and the listening-posts. The latter usually go in pairs, their duty to listen to the Germans in their trenches if they can approach close enough, to waylay enemy patrols, to uncover working parties. They are the spies, the doorkeepers, the watch-dogs, and altogether the uncomfortable ones of the company. They are selected for the things that make a good soldier—steadiness of nerve, intelligence, discrimination, knowledge of German quick-wittedness, and endurance. Which does not imply that all on listening-post possess these traits. If they do they are the more valuable.

After dark they crawl out over the parapet, often alone, conscious that their return is uncertain, aware that ahead of them stretches an interminable two hours of danger and discomfort. As close as they can get to the German trenches is their goal—through the German wire barricades if possible. And there they lie motionless, silent, low as the ground will let them, in water and mud. The deepest depression, where the mud and water await them, is their safest resting-place. To be against the skyline is certain exposure. And all the time the nervous German is sending up star-shells in search for such as he. He has orders not to shoot—as have all in No Man's Land at night—save as a last extremity. Three bombs he carries for protection if pressed, and a password for his own patrol partlies who are prowling about. In his hand may be the end of a string attached to a bell in the trench he has left, and by it he can say all he need say in a hurry.

For the rest he trusts to Providence and to the luck of the soldier. If the luck of the soldier is according to his deserts I know there is good fortune in store for such as V.

The patrol party is the listening-post in action. It combines the spying of the other with the beat of the policeman and the destructiveness of the soldier. Those of the regular patrol party are relieved of fatigue duty, but into the hours of darkness they cram thrills and danger enough at times to earn them more relief that they get.

Perhaps you, in your Morris chair to-night, can picture the weird work of the patrol in No Man's Land. Out there where not a finger dare show in daylight, where any careless bullet from either side may find its billet in him, where every second is a possible encounter with a thousand lurking dangers he cannot see, he prowls about in search of anything of value. He may crawl through the barb-wire before the German trenches and lie listening to the conversation of an enemy who fancies himself secure. He may run suddenly into a dark form, or a score of them, and have to hold his hand until he knows them as friend or foe. If friend there is the password. If foe—well, some quick thinking is necessary first of all. He must not reveal his location to either trench by bullet or bomb, except as a last resort. The knife or the bayonet are the safest weapons; failing these, bombs. The scene of a couple of patrol parties throwing bombs indiscriminatingly in the darkness contains all the mystery and excitement and uncertainty of a detective story with the possible solution the death of all concerned. When the patrol is out the trenches they left have orders not to fire towards the Germans; a friend is as vulnerable to a rifle bullet as a foe.

And yet the boys like it when there is no other excitement. There is action in it, the chance of getting even. There is about it that uncertainty that gives gambling its lure—and then there may be a V. C. To poke around in the darkness with the thrills running down your spine, uncertain what is ahead of you, whether a German, a clamorous machine-gun bullet, a sudden jab from a bayonet, or a six-foot hole filled with water, is more exciting than "playing the ponies" or dodging the police for a crap game. It even has its points over being caught in the open when the fog rises and shows you up to a thousand or two of snipers whose only interest in life is your death.

A patrol party usually consists of an officer, a sergeant, and six men, and a connection may be retained with the trenches by means of a bell at each end of the platoon.

Connection between the various parts of the army is vital. That is so obvious that its development has been affected less than any other department by the exigencies of this novel war. Communication between General Staff and army, between army and division, between division and brigade, between brigade and battalion, between battalion and company, between company and platoon, and even between scores of individuals off in hiding by themselves and their officers. And the guns must never lose touch with the infantry.

There is a system that keeps all these units together, and this war has culled out the useless details and leaned on those which have been found not wanting. The backbone of connection is the telephone. There are telephones everywhere on the field of battle, sometimes from far before the front line right back to General Joffre. Every tree may have its telephone, every shell hole, every dug-out; and every fence skeleton and hedge is certain to be the trail of wires that direct the conflict.

Wire layers and repairers are a part of every branch of the service, and their work is never complete. But the telephone is not always vocal. Back of battalion headquarters it may be a buzzer, and sometimes in front if the German lines are not too close. The buzzer can be tapped by the enemy more easily. The vocal telephone, when within some hundreds of yards of the enemy, is on metallic circuit for the purpose of retaining its secrets. And at the front end of the wire is the signaller.

Of course you have watched with more than ordinary interest the drilling in Canada of the signaller before he is sent overseas. You have seen a group of them, each with a pair of flags, wig-wagging to another group across a field. And you have been awed by the swiftness of gesticulation and the certainty of reply. It is there for you to see. So it would be for the enemy if it were in use where there is one.   .

The disillusioning feature of it is that these spectacular evolutions are nothing more than a course of calisthenics, so far as their usefulness to the present-day line of battle is concerned. The signaller is a signaller no longer. His flags are probably somewhere back in England with the rest of the junk of war waste. In the first place battles don't wait now for an officer in one field to wig-wag to an officer in another field that his guns are cutting up his friends instead of his enemies, or that the enemy is about to come over. In the second place signallers are not immortal—not in this life, and the supply would run out before a single flag had been raised. The enemy is not the least bit considerate when it comes to passing along messages by anticipated methods.

I am not certain of it offhand, but I should say that not a flag has waved in battle since 1914. It is a preparatory exercise for the consumption of open-mouthed civilians, and to convince those who enlist for the signal corps that they are signallers.

And the signallers have profited by it as well as the army. There is no straining of eyes, no nervous doubt, no mistake, no exposure. The signaller lies under cover taking the orders of his officer and transmitting them to their destination. And up at the front he has to do his own repairing of wires.

If anyone should guess at the miles of telephone wire that have been used in this war he would probably go mad with the immensity of it. At first the wire was a nice rubbered affair that cost so much per inch and when required elsewhere was taken up in order to limit the cost of the British army to $25,000,000 a day—as it is at the time of writing. Then common sense awoke. It struck someone that service was the thing, not polish; that a wire that could lie ignored when of no further use, at the saving of time and human life, was what this war needed. So they produced an enamelled wire that worked as well without costing enough to make it worth while to send a gang of men to remove it. Now there must be thousands of miles of cheap wire that has served its purpose, kicking about France for peace to collect and sell as souvenirs. It is everywhere over the ground, and everywhere it has been smashed to powder by a thousand guns.

Of course there is other wire. The nicely insulated variety is still used in the rear and removed with the removal of the units it feeds. Armoured cable is still in use for permanent posts and for headquarters. But where a flag used to deliver a message from the open on clear days in a couple of minutes, a bit of flimsy wire staked to the ground or run through a hedge transmits the same message more surely in a second. And seconds count.

There are times when the wires fail—when there is not time for their laying, when movement is too swift to be followed by the wire gang, when the bursting shells make dust of formal communication. It is then man comes into his own—with all the tight places and impenetrable barriers into which the carrying of despatches throws him.

Orders are carried under these conditions by three distinct bodies of orderlies. Back in comparative safety, although still within range of the guns and sometimes under excitement, the despatch riders whizz from headquarters to headquarters on motor-cycles. With the distances they have to cover and the large urgency of their reports, speed is important. Between the smaller units behind the lines bicycle orderlies do the work, their course facilitated by the lightness and mobility of their machines.

But while there is a certain glamour thrown on the work of the despatch riders, largely because they are the snobs of the despatch service and roar and rave and rattle about from point to point on mounts whose effectiveness seems to be based upon the noise they make and the speed they can maintain, there is a third branch of the service that performs the really dangerous, unsung work up at the front where the fury of the fight makes wire too mortal, where advance of small units has separated them from their companions, where the extreme pressure of the enemy makes immediate reinforcements and supplies necessary to the very life of the struggling men. Those who figure there are the battalion runners.

Were the services of the battalion runners narrated in full there would be books of bravery and sacrifice, of grim perseverance and reckless daring that would pretty nearly discount any other branch of the service. But because these young fellows work at sudden emergency, because they are too busy to demand their dues from the press, because they are few in number and small of size and come into contact only with a few officers, they pursue their imperilled path without a publicity agent.

I have talked to despatch riders whose many months of active service has earned nothing more serious for them than a spill at sixty miles an hour or thereabouts, or a hundred yard acquaintance with a "coal-box." But the despatch rider—like certain of the Flying Oorp before they have heard the sound of a gun—is primed with a luridness of description that savours of the exhaust of their motorcycles while carrying perhaps nothing more momentous than an invitation to a brother officer to come over and make up a table.

I have also talked with battalion runners who, having not the capacity for description, treat the most hair-raising experiences as the details of an ordinary day's work. In fact I have never yet drawn a story from a battalion runner except by the exercise of all my "pumping" ability. They are modest boys, trained in a silent, modest school, and their very isolation from the usual trench life deprives them of that ready exchange where the ordinary soldier is crammed with stock experiences.

Battalion runners seem to be selected for their smallness of size, their quickness of foot, their stubborness and determination, and their ability to go on to the end without being swerved aside by the incidents about them. The latter is the main qualification. The battalion runner must close his eyes and ears to everything but his destination. His work is not to fight except against the obstacles in his path; and nothing but death must stop him.

Battalion runners are the connecting links between units that have become separated. They must keep these units in touch, whether across the very mouths of German rifles or backward to the sources of relief and supply. Their orders are simply to get there, using every facility available. Usually they are on foot, sneaking along through shattered trenches, crawling from shell hole to shell hole, skirting danger by the merest hair's breadth to save time—running, creeping, lying down until danger is past, in silence and alone looking only to their own resources for the fulfilment of their purpose.

There are stories in my mind of the suffering and grim endurance and persistence of these despatch-bearers, that are almost monotonous in their lack of lurid detail. But anyone with some conception of conditions among the trenches may fill in without difficulty. I have heard of battalion runners on their way through enemy lines to reach a unit beyond, who were forced to worm along on hands and knees for miles and hours, always within touch of the foe. One runner hid for a week in the remains of a small woods, sneaking out at night to sustain himself on the pickings from the dead bodies that lay about. Germans by the hundreds were around him. But he delivered his message at the end—days after it was of any value. Often in their silent passage they meet the enemy on equally silent errands, and fight or run as the occasion or opportunity demands.

And such service is not rendered unscathed. They lie down and die out there where none knows what has happened, their message undelivered and their devotion unrewarded—and they are only casualties. The one thought in their minds is to last out to the moment when they can place the message in the hands they seek. Wounded to death they stagger on, and sink to final rest with the last words of the message on their lips. Even they hide their wounds that they might bear back the reply awaited.

A brave, tireless, defiant, silently suffering band of devoted soldiers, these runners who tempt to their own bodies the wounds they are trying to save their comrades. A modest group whose reward is in duty performed, not in the applause of the casual public. Some day their historian will earn them their deserts.

The next article of this series is entitled "The Non-Combatants", which describes the work of the vast number of men in the army who never see the firing-line.

The Non-combatants

By Lacey Amy
Part VII of With Canadians from the Front
From *The Canadian Magazine*, Vol. XLVIII March, 1917 No, 5.

All who don khaki are not fighters or Red Cross men. Another class has sprung up with the new conditions of war: the Pioneer Battalions, the sappers and miners and wirers. They are the labourers of the force, the men who take strange risks against which they can scarcely protect themselves. Their work is never finished, idleness is never more than enforced at the point of a gun. With the big guns roaring about them their duties continue, increase, oblivious to the fortunes of the struggle in which they indirectly take such an important share.

Day and night are the same to some of them. To others night and darkness provide the only protection they know. But some time their toil must be performed. The Pioneers are pioneers indeed, first on the new ground where the deserted, battered trenches of the enemy must be rebuilt without loss of time for their new occupants, always fighting against conditions that seem to conspire to impede them. Like the fighters, they are not fair-weather soldiers; but, unlike the soldiers, the resting enemy affords them no rest.

In the German army the Pioneers and sappers form an integral part of the combatant forces. When there is no fighting they are working. When their friends go "out over the top" they are in the thick of it. That is one reason why they are a larger proportion of the soldiers in the front lines. In the British army they are called on to fight only in extreme cases. In such a struggle as that at St. Julien, when the enemy was held up only by the grim grit of every man in the Canadian camps, they are able to prove that, under necessity, they can handle a rifle as well as a pick. But even the camp cooks and roustabouts were called into that affray. Every arm that could pull a trigger or throw a bomb figured in the repulse which added the grandest battle-page to Canadian history.

But these charmen of the army are not left to the charman's standing in society. The boys who make things possible, who make impossible the worst of the enemy's menaces, who offer to their friends that protection which could come from no other source, are not apt to be looked down on in an army where every man has his part—and it makes no difference whether he was a clergyman or a billiard marker. Digging trenches, piling up a parapet, gouging out a dug-out for others to enjoy, laying a trench mat, clearing the water and mud from about the soldiers' feet— it all gives them an importance which is appreciated at its real value in the scheme of things. And even back in camp they are not allowed to rust, for a camp is a huge house to look after. Then at night they may form a burying party, that evaded task of the soldier's daily life, with a chaplain mumbling reverently but hurriedly the service in the blackness of a cemetery within reach of the enemy's machine-guns.

Plug—plug—plug is the routine of the soldier who lifts pick and shovel as his share of the great war.

The miners are as real miners as those who seek coal or gold from the depths of the earth. Indeed many of them were miners in civilian life. The Maritime Provinces have supplied hundreds of miners from their coalfields, men inured to underground life and work, accustomed to the back flaying task in impure air, trained to play with gunpowder, to sense subterranean dangers, experienced in the demands of safety where an accident is certain death. England's miners have responded by the thousands, many of them engaged at their ordinary wages in a task that requires an expertness equal to that demanded of the army General.

Never, day or night, are the tunnelers of either side idle along those hundreds of miles of front. Down beneath the mud and cold of the trenches above, the snow and rain, the thunder of guns and the tearing of shells, the advance and retreat of struggling millions, the miners swing along foot by foot farther and farther towards the enemy, cutting the shafts and drifts and galleries that will some day play an important part in the defeat of the enemy. And the men above never forget it. To them the menace of the unsuspected mine is more terrible than a score of attacks.

Tunnels vary in size and length and shape as they do in the pursuits of peace. Usually about three feet wide and four to five feet high, they advance about a foot an hour, two miners using the pick while two others carry back the loosened earth.

If it is to be a long tunnel it will sink as far into the earth as sixty feet before striking its level. In that case it probably starts back in the supporting trenches and sinks either straight into the earth or by a slope. The extreme depth of a long tunnel is necessitated by the fact that an obstruction of water or rock is surmounted only by rising, and in a tunnel of a mile many upward deflections may be necessary. As it progresses it is shored up every three feet by timbers brought in by working parties during the night. The loosened earth is removed in sandbags that are used as parapet or emptied somewhere out of sight of the enemy. For the earth from a tunnel is recognizable, and the entire value of a mine is its surprise.

Over all these operations a mining officer, an engineer, has charge, performing the task as accurately according to plan as his facilities permit.

Some of these tunnels are the products of more than a year of unbroken work. As this is written there are at the front certain huge tunnels about which the soldiers speak in awed voices. Extending on and on, they pass beneath two, three, four enemy lines, even back beneath towns in which the enemy thinks himself secure, under artillery emplacements which will one day be marked only by a tremendous hole in the ground. When the time comes for advance these mines will play a part that will effect the results.

At the great fight at Hooge a German mine blew up almost an entire company of Canadians. The boys are going to exact retribution.

Four to eight hours at a stretch the miners toil underground, coming to the surface "for a blow" as the quality of the air and their experience demand. Fresh air is pumped in by bellows through pipes, but only the most modern ventilating system would purify the air of some of these larger tunnels.

And all the time an enemy mine may be near, awaiting the moment when it may be blown up with greatest damage. The only defence against a mine is a counter-mine. Groups of enemy miners may tunnel within hearing of each other, both feverishly seeking the advantage of level where the other may be destroyed. When the enemy's mining is suspected a counter-tunnel may be hurried out towards it and blown up in its path, thus blocking its progress by means of what is known as a *camouflet*.

Another kind of tunnel has proved itself especially serviceable to the Canadians. At an exposed point where a hill ranges behind the front lines a tunnel was dug beneath the hill to provide safe passage for the incoming and outgoing troops. Six feet in height, it is a luxury that has saved its hundreds of lives, for it prevents an exposed movement within easy range of an effective German artillery that here has every foot under fire.

A third variety of tunnel is that utilized as a listening-post. One of the wounded Canadian miners has told me that the strangest feeling he had at the front was when he lay only four feet or less beneath the feet of a trenchful of Germans, hearing them with perfect safety converse and laugh and play their musical instruments almost within reach of his hand. A charge of gunpowder would have blown up the entire company, but the spying value of the tunnel was greater than its destructive value. From that listening-post we were kept informed of every enemy movement in the immediate vicinity, with some knowledge of their gun emplacements, their working parties, their night patrols, and their suspicions of the movements of the enemy before them. There is always the chance that the conversation of the front line is within the hearing of the enemy.

The sappers are the privates of the Engineers. They take charge of fatigue parties for digging trenches, building parapets, laying trench-mats, guarding ammunition dumps and stores, and of the thousand and one duties for which men must be detailed. In most of these the knowledge of engineering, however slight, is of value.

The wirers have a particularly unpleasant job. Not so expert as the miners, they are, nevertheless, selected for this task which takes them always within reach of the enemy rifles and machine-guns, of flares, of bombing and patrol parties, of every sniper who looks out towards the lines for a chance shot. Barb wire, while it is a curse to friend and foe in the wrong place, is as necessary for protection and rest as the sentinels themselves. Its only place of usefulness is in the most dangerous part of the front, where only darkness offers protection to the men who stretch it. And the Germans have an unpleasant habit of turning loose a machine gun or two without provocation; and a machine gun may wipe out an entire company of wirers without knowing it. When the wirer goes out into No Man's Land he simply takes a big swallow —and his life in his hands. At the first sound of a Veery light, before it has had a chance to light up the ground, the wirer throws himself on his face or turns to stone and escapes notice by mere lack of movement.

His fate is less disagreeable to-day with the improvement in the style of fence. At first the posts were wooden, and had to be driven in. Even when they were made of iron in the next stage, they still were pounded in where noise was the last thing desired. The Germans first developed the new idea, the screw post, but the British quickly followed, the only difference in the two styles used being that the British posts did not have the arms that were a characteristic of the German variety. Now a wiring party goes out into the danger zone and works in silence. The posts are four feet high and eight feet apart, with a low post midway between. The barb wire, which at first was wired to the wooden posts, then strung through poles in the early iron posts, is now simply looped over hooks on the posts. From high post to high post it runs, with other wires proceeding downwards to the low posts, thus making a network impossible to pass through without cutting.

Comment has long been made on the maze of wires that protects the German lines, the deduction being that the enemy is much more afraid of surprise attacks than are our men, so nervous, in fact, that he is willing sometimes to wire himself in as well as wire our soldiers out. And patrol and listening-post is considered to be an integral feature of the British war scheme.

The strain of continued wiring must be tremendous. S., a Toronto-born lad who enlisted in the West, was sent from the trenches to hospital with a complication of diseases, among them being a weakness of the heart. Arriving in England for treatment, he fumed at the enforced inaction, for, although feeling at times almost as well as ever, he was ordered to bed. He knew it was unlikely that he would see the trenches again, and back in Canada a very sick sister and mother called to him to return. It seemed to him, too, that only in Canada would there be relief to the lung trouble that was one of his ailments.

Of course his only chance was to remain in bed, an order which he consistently ignored at every opportunity. He was a dark, suspicious-eyed fellow, fostering the idea that the world was against him, and to every effort at restraint he opposed a watchful silence or an explosive disgust. The knowledge that came to him gradually that the doctors were not frank with him increased his insubordination, and finally one evening I undertook to put his case frankly before him. It was a seemingly useless task, for when I called the next two nights he was out. On the fourth evening I was prevented from visiting the hospital, and a message was delivered to me from him that he was remaining in bed at last. I understood. For a week I saw him every day, and for another week he stuck faithfully to his word. Then he was allowed up, and to give himself some interest in life he established a barbershop in the hospital. It brightened him up wonderfully. And there he remained, seeing ahead of himself in the end a reasonable recovery that could be attained only with extreme care.

His weak constitution and bad family record were scarcely the foundations on which to build a wirer's career.

Of course there are thousands of others in khaki who not only have not fought the enemy but have not even seen them, who could scarcely be called soldiers in any sense of the word. Many of these have landed in the non-combatant service from choice. For instance, the Canadian War records Office in London was filled with them, until a "man-power board" yielded to public clamour and cleaned a lot of them out for the work for which they were supposed to enlist. But "man-power boards" are more for the public eye than for real "combing-out", and still many continue to draw good pay without more danger than threatens in the life of London. There have been, too, in these offices many who were not permitted to go to the front, because their faithfulness to the work in hand made their presence in London desirable. What they suffered from was the quality of their work. The young fellow who loafed on his job and filled no essential place in the offices was—unless he had the "pull"—cleaned out for active service, while those who were eager to do everything they touched with all their energies were put down as "indispensable", although they were usually the ones who had enlisted to be real soldiers. In addition there were a number upon whom sickness fell before they could cross the Channel. So that not by any means all the clerks in the War Records Office were shirkers.

Of the didn't-want-to's I came across an interesting example who for many months had succeeded in evading discovery. He was admitted to the hospital where I met him with what appeared to be shellshock. It was a well-defined case. I saw him first seated on a bench in the blazing sun (of which England had experienced none for weeks previously) but in his surly, cynical face was a hopelessness and disgust with life that seemed to call for sympathy. His right knee thrown over his left twitched spasmodically and he watched it with sneering contempt and disgust.

From the first word I found him "fed up" with everything—the many hospitals he had been in, the weather, the state of his health, the food and treatment he had received at everyone's hands. He was explosive in language, irritable, almost vicious, with a face from which every gleam of pleasure seemed to have taken permanent leave. At times it was impossible to get a word out of him until some impulse started him, when he would hiss and sputter out his anathema until it was considered wise to keep the poisons out of his reach. The only treatment seemed to be to rouse his interest in something outside himself, and at first he was put on the mess. For a few days he improved, and then he began to complain of the clatter of the dishes. He was set at gardening, but something or other there did not agree with him and he was put to making chicken coops. For a few weeks the young chickens did seem to be working a cure.

I came to understand his case and the reason for his eternal grouch, as well as for his transference from hospital to hospital. He had not only never been at the front but he had tried every means to escape being sent. At Shorncliffe his leg was injured by being thrown from a horse, but his "shellshock" was sheer fear. In the hospital where he was undergoing treatment for his leg the inmates quickly diagnosed his case and laid themselves out to make him undergo some, at least, of the suffering, even though he never got to the trenches. They piled on him such terrible stories of the life in the trenches, the suffering, the danger, the misery and injuries that he developed shellshock without having heard a big gun. It is an established fact that the boys who have been in the trenches have nothing but contempt for the khaki-clad pseudo-soldiers who prefer a safe job in England to taking a term in the active fighting.

Of the other kind who were prevented from reaching the front one whom we will call R. is a good example. R., a Westerner, had enlisted with the C.A.M.C. Always before him he held the picture of the good he might do as a stretcher-bearer up in No Man's Land. After very little training he was sent to England and there his training stopped. His earnestness and indefatigability earned for him right away one of those positions of drudgery that come to the faithful, in order that some officer may have at his beck and call the best workers in the army. He became a batman to an officer, and such a good one that his delivery to the active forces was not to be thought of. In the course of many changes he reached a convalescent home, not as a patient but as one of the staff whose duties were to scrub and sweep and clean and perform other tasks within the powers of wounded soldiers unfit for the front. Transferred to another convalescent home, he came to my notice. He was never idle. No need to point out what needed attention; R. always saw it and attended to it. When the ordinary of the staff orderly failed, he filled in his time in a little garden he commenced to make in waste ground.

He was too good for the trenches, of course, said the officers.

He became a silent lad, moving about his work with a wordless suffering behind his patience that was pathetic. It was in a moment of confidence that I obtained his story. He had never been "crimed," never been even lectured save when he pleaded to get to the front. Strong and cleareyed, he was at first sight the very man to have about anywhere. Had he dared he would have removed the red cross from his arm, "for," said he, "anyone can do this work. I thought I might be of use out there at the front," he moaned. "They told me they needed stretcher-bearers when I enlisted."

I was able to obtain for him his wish, and the last word I had from him, written in a Y.M.C.A. hut at the front, was the gratitude of a happy soldier at last within sound of the guns. The flotsam in the eddies and back currents of military red tape and discipline is sometimes as pathetic as the suffering of the wounded and nerve-stricken.

Another, a Russian, who enlisted in Prince Albert, Saskatchewan, came over to England as a gunner, full of the enthusiasm that so often characterizes that branch of the service. When about ready to leave for the front, at Shomcliffe his gun backfired. Once before it had done the same without serious injury to any of the crew, but the second time it caught five of them. The other four recovered, but the Russian's heart had been too badly tampered with. In the hospital he struggled hard with his malady. Time after time as the medical officer inspected the boys he put on the best face he knew how, but the trained ear heard the murmur of the weak heart and turned the Russian back. Long since I lost track of him but at the last he was becoming reconciled to return to Canada without a taste of that for which he had enlisted.

As sad as any are the cases of those who took sick in the training camps in England through no fault of their own. The exposure of that first camp at Salisbury Plains will stand for many years a discredit to the authorities. How many of the boys contracted through it pneumonia or rheumatism, tuberculosis, kidney trouble or the other diseases resultant from such outrageous mud and exposure I do not know. That any of them came through it is surprising. English weather, combined, perhaps with a certain recklessness on the part of the boys, has claimed a toll that has decreased as experience taught the best methods of combatting it. So that to-day the Canadian soldier who has no chance to reach France is becoming a rarity. In that stands the protection of these who would be real soldiers.

Woman and the War

By Lacey Amy
Part I of 'England in Arms'
From *The Canadian Magazine*, XLIX, May, 1917 No. 1.

To appraise with fairness the participation of the English woman in the war requires some acclimatization on the part of the Canadian. My earliest impressions were of a gentler sex, only a stage removed from the actual conflict, who would benefit from a lesson in work from her Canadian sister. Later experience, while it may not have altered greatly my opinion in that respect, has subdued it and shaded it through a better understanding of relative values. Justice demands the inclusion in the perspective of more than the mere manual or mental performances of the English woman.

It is impossible, I think, that in any other country the stress of an extended war could break so strikingly into the career of the non-combatant sex. Indeed, England, from top to bottom, has been torn and revolutionized by sheer necessity, as no other country need have been under similar circumstances. That is the natural concomitant of a system of distinct class boundaries. A short war might have been struggled through without the social cataclysm that has struck England; but such a struggle as the present one levelled social fences as a part of victory. The high were brought down and the low raised.

The wealthy were forced to the level of some sort of labour by legislation, by popular demand and custom, by a real desire to assist, and even by the necessity of earning a living. The poor were lifted to the plane of profitable labour by the pressing demand for their hands.

What this levelling process means to England may be partly estimated without living through the metamorphosis. And it was among the women of the nation that "class" was, before the war, developed to its highest point and maintained by a determined tradition of aristocracy and by a submissive, conventional proletariat. Nothing in human nature exceeded the chasm between the "lady" and her servant. There were, it is true, the closest bonds of fidelity and loyalty, but nothing ever for a moment permitted the two representatives of the extreme classes to meet on a level of humanity.

The result on the English woman of the better class was a traditional refusal to perform the most ordinary services for herself. Only a few days before the writing of this, the death of the Duke of

Norfolk brought out this marvellous evidence in the daily press of his "unselfish and unaffected nature"—that, entering a room in his house to receive a visitor and finding the grate unlighted, "he knelt at once down and lit it himself, taking immeasurable pains to make it burn quickly and brightly." A woman of any class would no more have thought of "kneeling down" to do anything—except for her prayers—than she would have carried a parcel from the store to her waiting car. And the English woman, from the lower classes to the top, never learns the simplest branches of household art unless circumstances force her to it.

Thus it was that she was faced with a catastrophe. To be useful at a time when every hand and brain counted, the upper classes must overthrow a tradition that had become fixed in the nation's creed. And the lower grades of society were bewildered by a condition wherein they counted even more than their superiors, and where their country was willing to pay for it.

The response of the English women, therefore, cannot be dissociated from the upheaval in the social system. Where the Canadian woman simply pitched in and knit socks or made bandages or organized others for the work, the English woman had first to reorganize the whole social fabric of which she was the most adamantine part. If an aristocrat, she had never had a knitting needle in her hands; she had never moved a muscle for anything a servant might perform for her. If a plebeian, she was forced to be a party to a levelling process never anticipated in her wildest dreams, and to do it without disrupting the social co-operation necessary for the profitable fulfilment of the sphere she and her sisters of all classes were called upon to fill for the very salvation of the Empire.

I have elaborated on what might be considered merely an introduction, because nothing done by the women of England can be considered by a Canadian in the light of Canadian experience alone.

This description of conditions precluding complete participation by the English woman in the war work open to her frees me for a general statement without prejiidice, omitting for the moment consideration of her handicaps. I am prepared to say that not all the better class women of England have done in the aggregate what a tenth their number of Canadian women would have accomplished in the same time. They have not taken to knitting for several reasons. Those who are keenly anxious to do effective war work without delay have not the patience to learn; and those who have but yielded to the prevailing fashion do not see in quiet knitting that which will return them full credit for their energy. Also, there are still those in whose mind continues the almost unsuspected impression that knitting is for a lower class. In a whole year I have seen only one English woman knitting.

It is the women of the lower classes who have responded in a manner that calls for no qualifications, no conditions, and not alone for the high wages their work now brings them.

I will go further. Women in England (even to-day, although the past few months have seen wonderful strides in this respect) have never been organized for that profitable production which commenced in Canada with the outbreak of the war. There again the social lines are responsible, not thoughtlessness. The great middle class (and there are three or four grades in it) looks to the levels above for its cue. But the early work of the aristocrats was in the way of spectacular operations that took them into hospitals, in England or in France, through organizations of their own kind; and there the middle class was unable to follow. Even to-day the opportunity of sharing in the immediate care of the wounded in hospital is obtainable only by influence; it is a real victory, a social distinction. For Ladies and Honourables have from the first hankered even to get down on their knees on the front steps of a hospital (the very depths of menial labour) and apply the brush.

The result was a complete lack of organization among the middle classes. I personally know whole suburbs where, up to the middle of last year, not an organized effort was being made. The churches were not the centres of working parties, as in Canada. There were no local associations, no gatherings of friends. It was partly owing to the fact that it is a London custom not to know one's next door neighbour; and there is not the church fraternity that prevails in Canada.

Having said that, I wish once more to warn my readers not to deny the English women their dues. During the last six months they have learned more hard work than the country has known in centuries, and only now is the one great central organization, the Women's Department of National Service, getting to work. It is impossible, too, not to be astonished at the whole-souled, enthusiastic efforts of thousands of well-born women from the first days of the war. Their sacrifice has been greater than a Canadian can imagine, for the reason that with their manual labour fled a traditional prejudice, an ancestral idleness, the instincts that have for ages determined their social level. Many a social leader has ruined the grace and colour of her hands for life, many a titled heroine has willingly stooped to work she would have asked only of her lowest servant. And the early hysteria of publicity has long since lost its attraction, so that now it is only the assistance they are giving that counts. I hope that nothing I have said, or will say, may rob these women of the glory that is theirs.

And with my respect for these iconoclasts goes a reverence for the hundreds of thousands of munition workers who risk their lives every day, the great majority of them taking as keen a satisfaction in their share of the shell-making and filling as thrills their "boys" at the front when one of the products of female hands bursts in a German trench. When the great explosion occurred in London, there was no reluctance among the women to continue their dangerous toil. Within the following week the Ministry of Munitions advertised for 30,000 women workers among high explosives, and the response was keener than it had ever been. I believe that the very extent of the danger brought home to them the value of the risk they were taking, its importance in the winning of the war. As I stood at the one exit from the scene of that explosion and saw the hundreds of women stagger out, wounded, bearing everything they possessed in the world, there was no fear in their faces, no mental evidences of having passed through a tragedy. And within the week the fit among them were again working with the T.N.T., the great explosive of this war.

The amazing discovery of the war is the adaptability of woman to tasks never before attempted by her, tasks that have been so exclusively confined to man's sphere that nothing but a prime necessity would have offered them to the other sex. When the idea of female substitution was first broached it was accepted that there were definite limits to its utilization. Only in certain tried, conventional positions could a woman be placed to relieve men for the front. At first she was placed in offices. After that it was considered wise to proceed cautiously to prevent disorganization and wasted effort. But gradually the insistent call for more men in the trenches encouraged experiments which brought bewildering results.

To-day even the Prime Minister's secretary is a woman.

There is not a trade or occupation in the varied industries of England, save those few in which is necessary the highest trained skill—trades which occupy so very few men as to be negligible—where woman is not proving that, with the necessary physique and commonsense, she is capable of becoming an effective substitute for man during the trying phases of the war. That does not intend to imply that she performs all her tasks as efficiently as man, for the training and instincts of generations cannot be altered in a year or two; but her unsuspected applicability has lightened the burden of war and succeeded in breaking down barriers whose existence was not conducive to the greatest development of any race. Without the women of England the war would never be won.

The streets of London reveal this diverse usefulness of the gentler sex at every step. Dressed in pantaloons and long coats they clamber up uncertain ladders to clean windows. They drive delivery wagons, horse and motor. They act as conductors on omnibus, tram, and underground. They run elevators, carry messages, deliver and collect mail, push milk and bread carts, clean the railway carriages, light the street lamps, substitute for chauffeurs by the hundreds, and form almost the entire staff at theatres, restaurants and hotels. They have even encroached on that profession of the male "crock", the sandwich-board carrier.

Into these urban occupations they slid with no sound of rubbing or jar. But it was when they began to dribble into the heavier, more skilled trades that the nation began to rub its eyes.

The necessity for brute strength does not exclude them. I have seen them handling huge beer kegs with more vim and speed than their brothers. They load brick and perform porter's work in hundreds of establishments. In munition factories they lift shells and wheel trucks, and grumble less than the sex built for heavy work. They toil on the docks with the surliest, roughest men in civilized life.

When women secured a chance to exhibit their diverse accomplishments in the skilled trades they surprised themselves, their employers, the men who worked on the next benches, and the nation. Early in the war they were taking the place of painters, and the differences are not evident to the inexpert. As carpenters they were slow to develop, partly because of the close corporation they had to fight in the Carpenters' Union and partly because of their instinctive fear of sharp tools. Now the authorities are sending them to France by the score to erect soldiers' huts. They make roads better than the old men who undertook the work when the younger generation was called up.

From the mechanical arts of the factory they were long excluded by the unions, most of which had agreements with the Asquith Government that they should not be interfered with by the recruiting officers. But again necessity interfered and a scheme of substitution once inaugurated they showed themselves so amazingly proficient that the men are ashamed of themselves. In the munition factories they manipulate the most complicated machinery, of late even doing their own repairing. They do almost all the work in connection with the construction of aeroplanes. On the Tyne are female blacksmith's helpers. They do electrical wiring, chip, clean, and paint warships, construct turbines, make lifeboats, assemble the parts of barometers and compasses.

Women have revolutionized the army. The old folly of male cooks has been relegated to the past. In opposition to every tradition of the British army women are being taken on to manage messes as fast as they can be secured. This is principally the result of enforced economy, and the other benefits have come unexpectedly. Up to the third year of the war it was a tradition of the army that economy in the mess was undignified, contrary to every precedent upholding the honour of the soldier. Then it was discovered that the waste from a battalion would keep another. Reforms were attempted early, but results were disappointing. Convention demanded that they should be disappointing. The men suffered and the saving was paltry. The introduction of female cooks altered everything. Not only is there a real economy, but the men are better fed and better satisfied, there is less graft, and discipline is more easily maintained.

The number of women who had responded to their nation's call by the end of 1916 is revealing. Although at the time of writing the new National Service is but started, the many organizations of the first thirty months of the war had replaced almost a million men with women. It is an interesting point that it required only 988,500 women to take the places of 933,000 men. But these figures should not be taken too literally as an absolute comparison of values. Many industries have been curtailed or closed; but on the other hand many have been enlarged.

All told, there are estimated to be more than four and a quarter million of paid women workers engaged in regular occupation, and in this number are not included the voluntary hundreds of thousands, the many nurses and part-time workers. Two and a half millions are in factories. The 2,000 in Government establishments before the war have grown to 120,000, and the rate of increase is several thousands a month. In commercial occupations are 750,000, in professional occupations 82,500, in banking and finance the number employed has increased from 9,500 to 46,500. In hotels and public amusements there are two hundred thousand, in agriculture 140,000, in army messes 2,000. And so the list continues, growing so rapidly that figures hold even approximately only for a few days. By the time this is read there will be another quarter of a million at work of real value for the progress of the war. The call for substitutes for the men behind the lines in France is bringing women in throngs to the organization headquarters.

Some industries have turned over their men entirely to the military authorities. One railway has built up its female staff from seventy to five thousand. There are 35,000 nurses. The post-office employs 65,000. The London telephone service, before the war employing men largely, is now "manned" by women. The London Gas, Light and Coke Company employs 1,100. In ten months 1,655 women conductors have passed through the general omnibus training school. The latest sphere for them is driving taxi-cabs, and their record here will be watched with more than ordinary interest as revealing better than any other occupation their fitness for work that requires presence of mind and mechanical efficiency on short notice. Although they are not yet on the streets, the men have threatened to strike if their domain is invaded.

One of the developments of the later months of the war is the demand of the women for pay commensurate with their work. This applies not alone to the working classes who are accustomed to pay for services, but to all. It has been brought about by the discovery that paid work is most satisfactory, both for discipline and reliability; and thousands of those who offered themselves in the early months without reward find themselves unable to continue thus. There is, too, a feeling that while some are making fortunes from the war, there can be no reason in others exhausting themselves for larger returns to profiteers.

In agriculture women, while unfitted to replace men, individual for individual, have proved themselves adaptable to conditions their sex instinctively dislikes. Scoffed at as workers of the land, they have conquered by sheer determination and pluck. The sliminess and muck of the English climate, and the odious class distinctions from which the farmer's help suffers most, have failed to erect a barrier against the gentler sex. The farmer has resisted their encroachment into his organization from the first, yielding only when it became women or no crops. In the early stages of substitution many incompetent women offered themselves for that which afforded the greatest publicity as most uncongenial to their sex. The result was disastrous to the farms. These city-bred and better class women quickly wearied of the life or were dismissed as inefficient, and for a time only the rough, or country-bred were available. Lately the necessity for greater food production brought into the fields those untrained women who promise to do their best because of the very fact that they offer themselves when the nature of the work is better known. The great obstacle of insufficient pay for the women to keep themselves is now overcome by a Government measure that sets the minimum at twenty-five shillings.

Policewomen are new in England. In their regular capacity as assistants of the men they are proving themselves of real service in London in the handling of the demi-monde. In outside towns, however, their experience has varied. Some municipalities are pleased, others have dispensed with them after trial. As in other spheres, success depends upon the individual. Not long ago the Government advertised for three hundred policewomen for munition factories, their duties being largely to maintain discipline among the female workers and to prevent the introduction of dangerous elements among the high explosives. Almost a thousand applied. The pay ranges from two pounds to two and a half a week, uniform not found.

Of course, the great demand for the women workers has been in the munition factories. Here, from a small beginning, the number has increased to more than half a million and their duties include everything but the most severe lifting. As a rule, too, men are still employed to manage the floors and to repair machines, but even they are being replaced. It is unnecessary that thousands of fit young men be concealed in munition factories, for the experience has been that women do their work better than the men. However, many foremen are still prejudiced against them, and here and there are managers who fear to lose a few pounds by extending the substitution. The unions, too, stand behind the men. Yet the experience of France has been that the introduction of female labour has increased each worker's daily output of shells from three to nine.

Many factories never cease work, Sundays and certain hours of day or night being filled by "lady" workers.

Naturally, with such diversity of demand and response, the calibre of the work performed by women varies. The paid worker must, as a rule, earn her money—except perhaps in the Government Departments, where thousands of extravagantly dressed women and girls crowd in each other's way, report late, leave early, and go by taxicab to an expensive restaurant for a luncheon lasting an hour and a half. Not every custom can be overthrown, even in three years of war.

It is in the realm of voluntary work that are exhibited heights of wasted energy and disorganization. The first rush of the better classes for war-work was to the hospitals and canteens. In the former their success depended upon their influence and position in society, until their frequent uselessness impelled the Government to clean them out of France and limit their duties in England. During the first six months of the war the ambition of the titled woman seemed to be to get her picture into the illustrated papers in nurse's costume. The uniform may have been flattering, but the work was not of a nature to be forgotten once the picture had appeared. By scores and hundreds they succumbed to the drudgery, and general inefficiency completed the exodus. After that it dawned upon England that a title did not preclude real nursing ability or working sense; and there are still hundreds of wealthy, blooded women in the hospitals of France and England performing work their friends never suspected them to be capable of.

But where the rush of influence was so clamorous there was introduced a system that still prevails. The hospitals of England are staffed by part-time workers who are permitted the luxury of work only one or two half-days a week, on account of the numbers who desire to be connected with the work for the wounded. The result is that they never learn much, never take their work seriously, and exhaust their nervous energy and strength by too many outlets. There are thousands of English women flitting about between half a dozen employments, criticism being silenced by the fact that they accept nothing for their services. And yet most of them would be willing to confine themselves to one task were the custom to be altered. I do not think it will alter, except as the Government takes over war-work, as it has lately taken over the canteens.

Another unfortunate feature of English organizations is that everybody must be headed by a title. It seems impossible to operate, however necessary the work, however honest the organization, however technical the duties, without the committee of management consisting of titled women. The result is easily imagined. There is glaring lack of organization, wastefulness and incompetence, without any effort to improve. The principle is not peculiar to England, although its development there is most complete. Canteens, charitable associations, women's employment bureaus—everything is handled by a representative of the nobility who never in her life had to think of economy of money and time and energy. It was this spectacle, I imagine, that induced the Government to step in and put an end to unofficial canteens in munition factories and military camps, managed by volunteers.

I have in mind a large canteen organization. So extravagantly managed was it—although not a worker received a cent—that it was unable to compete with the multiple London restaurants. It paid exorbitant prices for its supplies, was defrauded on every hand by its tradespeople, and even cleanliness was a stranger to it. And yet, as one of the greatest canteen organizations of the war, it was lauded extravagantly. Its workers were all "ladies". Many of them refused to wash and clean. Often they turned up at the booths with their maids to do the work, while they sat and looked on, their cars waiting for them, to tire of even that exertion. "Bubble-and-squeak", and "toad-in-the-hole" were to them hideous concoctions beneath their notice. They came and went when they pleased. And always the rules of precedence had to be strictly observed. Yet some of those women are glorying to-day in a knowledge of work they hitherto considered fit only for servants.

The honourary secretary of an economy league furnished through a London paper the other day a sample menu for those who would observe the food rations set down by the Food Controller. In great detail she described the food requirements of herself, her husband, one child, and seven servants, and London patted her on the back as a real economist for sacrificing patriots to imitate.

Of late the largest canteen organization, although headed by two titled women, has definitely decided not to accept ladies as workers.

The effects of this wartime work on England's women are as yet uncertain in their details, but that there will be tremendous changes in the country after war is certain. I am inclined to think that some of the best results will show themselves in the men. A breach in the walls of class prejudices and distinctions has been made. Women of all classes are working side by side and discovering that, after all, William the Conqueror gave to his most intimate friends very little of real service to their descendants. To produce a shell to kill Germans is worth more than the bluest blood of the centuries. The upper classes are learning to appreciate the lower, and the lower are on the way to asserting their position. One result that will change things in future is the growing independence of woman. Not only has she proven her worth, but a real wage and the ability to earn it have given her self-respect. I do not think that the munitioneer will stand the proprietary, often bullying, tone of the average Englishman to his women.

The fact is that the munitioneer has done better work and more of it than the men, with less absenteeism, less restricting unionism, less complaining, and a greater interest in output. Foremen who have overcome their prejudices frankly state their preference for the female worker, and the tone of the factories has been distinctly raised by the introduction of women and their welfare workers.

There is, of course, another side— the hardening influence of competitive labour. I am inclined to alter my first impressions on that point. Among the lower classes the effect will be improving, and even if the women of the upper grades of society are introduced to a life where female "modesty" is not a rite, a country is better built up by its labouring people than by its aristocrats.

Woman's suffrage stands to be affected. Undoubtedly many anti-suffragists among the men have been converted to votes for women. But it is argued that because some women have proved their capacity is no more a claim to woman's suffrage than the equally evident fact of incapacity in others is an argument against it. And even the children of England are working harder than millions of women.

There is no other conclusion than that England's women have provided the surprise of the war. The working classes have shown themselves a real factor in the winning of the war, able and eager to do their utmost. And even the nobility have overcome much to perform a share that, while in the aggregate it may seem inconsequential to democratic Canada, is relatively a sacrifice to them not equalled by those whose training permits them to be more useful.

In the June Number there will be another article by Mr. Amy on "England in Arms".

The Farmer and the War

By Lacey Amy
Part II. of 'England in Arms'.
From *The Canadian Magazine*, June 1917.

No one in England has been more intimately affected by the war than the farmer. No one in England will, in the long run, profit so completely.

"No doubt the State showed a lamentable indifference to the importance of agricultural industry, the very life of the nation. No civilized country spent less on agriculture, or even spent as little on it, directly or indirectly, as we did."

In that frank confession before the House on a memorable day in February, nineteen-seventeen, Lloyd George, faced by a startling shortage of food as the result of the condition he now deplored, supported by the ready assent of a people who had, for the first time in its history, been forced to weigh its allowance, sounded a nation's remorse. Ahead stared the menacing future of a struggle with a ruthless foe that was attacking in England's most vulnerable spot. Behind were generations of neglect of the only industry that could surely save her in her extremity. Ahead lay even the uncertainty of a victory that might have been assured had England not so immutably set her course by a plan whose blindness was now recognized perhaps too late. "Seventy to eighty per cent. of our wheat has been imported," groaned the Premier. "Our food stocks are low, alarmingly low— lower than they have ever been within recollection." And a nation, paying the penalty of its own folly, grimly bent its tardy efforts to reforming the system, to remodeling its ideas of national industry and national life.

Hitherto the English farmer, in a country where man is classified largely by the work he does, moved on the lowest plane. He fulfilled no vital function of national existence. He lived on suffrance. His only recognized function was to render profitable some insignificant part of the huge tracts owned by wealthy landlords, and to keep them in shape for the latter's amusements. He was little more than a servant of the landlord from whom he rented his land—for he seldom owned it. Generation after generation his family grovelled and dug, hopelessly, almost stupidly, ground down by the system that deprived him of every incentive of ambition. His sons who were worth while left him and sailed for the Colonies, where a man might be a man and still be a farmer, where the limits of the scale, social and financial, depended only on a man's capacity.

There is another "farmer" in England, the landlord owner who never handled a hoe or stirred a spadeful of earth or harnessed a horse. His voice swells in the House of Commons, on the public platform, in rural organizations. The other day a London newspaper displayed a letter from a "Farmer" protesting against the cry for more cultivation when labourers were unavailable owing to the demands of the Army. On his 800 acre farm, he lamented, he had but sixteen hands, and the land was idle for want of workers. But the letter was sent from one of the most exclusive and expensive clubs in London. There are thousands like him in England—men who call themselves farmers but never farm, who bewail the dearth of help but scorn to remove their own coats. That is not the farmer of whom I am going to speak.

The English farm was but a corner of a large sporting estate. Where tens of acres were tilled hundreds were left wild for the deer, the fox, the pheasant, the rabbit to multiply for the sport of the landlord. Or parks and paddocks in the best locations represented the owner's keenest concern. Deer browsed off the fields, and foxes and pheasants grew fat on the farmers' work that the lord of the manor might find his sport at his door. And the sufferer from their depredations dare not shoot them. The huntsmen galloped across his fields in pursuit of the fleeing fox; they left open his gates and controlled the heights of his fences to the capacities of their horses. And the farmer had no redress. Even after two and a half years of war, when game had multiplied through lack of hunters until the farmers' best efforts threatened to be nullified, it was only against keen opposition in the House that they were given the right to shoot the game that was assisting the enemy to cut down the nation's subsistence. A conservative country fought to the last ditch any change that favoured the farmer against the idle landlord even when the latter's food was at sake with the former's.

England was a nation of sportsmen, of financiers, of shopkeepers. What need of the farmer? Were there not unending fleets of merchant ships to fetch the food the islands needed? Was there not the Navy to protect them against the world's attacks in their passage? Folly, England declared, to break up the fields that formed the amusement of the wealthy. England would always be mistress of the seas. The rest of the world might be the world's granary.

The result was inevitable. Smaller and smaller grew the farms, tighter and tighter the areas of tilled fields. The farmer did not develop for there was not the room. He made no experiments; he was not supposed to. Experiment was not for his class. He stuck to the beaten track of his grandfather, without a vision of better things. And his sons, disgusted, revolutionary, left him. Gradually land that had raised its average of thirty bushels of wheat passed into the interminable pasture that covers England. Five millions of acres ceased to cater to the needs of the people. For seventy miles round London there is no farming. Down in Kent there are broken acres set out with hop poles, but scarcely anywhere within that area, especially to the south and east and west, do growing fields of grain gladden the eye. No prairie was ever more unproductive. Golf links everywhere, rolling sweeps of meadow land adorned with a few sheep and cattle, rising heights of glorious parks—a dream of gentle, beautiful landscape, but useless, utterly useless to a country surrounded by water.

That was England up to 1917. Now the scene is changing. "The plough is our hope," admitted Lloyd George, with that candid note of apology that promises bright things for the future. "The war at any rate has taught us one lesson—that the preservation of our essential industries is as important a part of the national defence as the maintenance of the Army and Navy." And in that sentence rang hope to the dulled farmer, the emancipation of an industry that had been choked almost to extinction. The Island Kingdom had awakened to the fact that no nation can repudiate the essentials of life and thrive, even under its ordinary contingencies.

Yet even to-day there are Free Trade enthusiasts—so far publicly expressing themselves only in the House of Lords—who contend that had the farmer been protected, had he been encouraged, England would not have possessed its 12,500,000 tons of shipping when the war broke out. No one has troubled to reply. The outcome of the next three months will answer—it is answering now.

The war had been in progress almost two years when Mr. Asquith, then Premier, rose in the House and assured it that there was no need for worry. The submarine peril had been overcome; England might continue to import its food stuffs with perfect confidence in its future. There might be shortages here and there in certain luxuries, but the granaries of the world were at the nation's door. It pleased England, the conservative, that it need not change. But a very few months later, while still there was no submarine ruthlessness, the Premier had risen to alter his tone. Wheat was climbing to unprecedented heights. The condition of the market was proving that, even should the country not starve, there was little profit in leaving itself in the hands of foreigners, whether the seas were free or not. But it was left to the Premier demanded by a people who had begun seriously to doubt to face the real crisis of England's policy.

Of course every industry and occupation in England considers that it has been especially selected to bear the brunt of the war. But labour and food production, the two great sources of victory, quite as vital as the Army and the Navy, can bear only a certain amount without the entire nation paying the penalty. Both responded to the early call of the recruiting officers with a zeal that spoke well for their loyalty. The farming communities were unevenly affected, as were the towns. In certain districts the patriotism was of such an intense nature that farmers were shorn of their assistance almost to the point of stopping production. The Derby scheme took many more. One hundred and eight thousand farm-hands enlisted voluntarily.

In the early stages there was no thought of selection. England must have an Army, wherever it was obtained. Kitchener had to raise a million men almost by the stroke of the wand. Nothing else mattered but that France should have the instant support of its most powerful but most unprepared ally. Even when the pressing urgency of men grew less insistent there was no fear of the depletion of the farms. Where some sections had enlisted en masse others had not felt the call; the farmers thought that somewhere in England was labour enough. Their patriotism was more sensitive than their purses. All England was too sure of itself, too confident that history would be repeated without seriously disturbing the country 's plan of life.

But when conscription ruthlessly took the fit, the loose labour market was thinned out and the farmer had nowhere to turn to make up his deficiency. So he did the thing that had for many years come so easy to him— turned his growing grain fields into grass lands. One of the difficulties was the English system of labour. Farms and private houses, factories and stores, are in ordinary times manned by an army of help that has learned to confine itself to its specified duties. A house that in Canada would be content with two servants, in England employs five. A farm that would be worked in Canada by two men, in England is shorthanded without seven or eight—probably with more intensive farming. It is an extravagance of labour from which there is much suffering now. And so many farms were devoted to fancy crops that required additional hands. Nevertheless the condition had to be taken as it was, and while it is changing rapidly under necessity, there is loss of energy in the process.

The work of the Tribunals appointed to decide on exemptions from the Army did little to improve matters. Some ignored every plea of the farmer and took his assistant. Others refused to make the farmer organize his work that fewer helpers might do it. Thus there were farm-hands to spare in places, and land that could not be worked in others. It depended upon the direction of one's vision whether one condemned the Tribunals as careless of the Army or of the nation's food. In general it was natural that the military representatives who appeared before these official bodies should insist on the farmer as most suited by his outdoor, severe work for the harsh life of the trenches.

In the fall of 1916 the country could no longer ignore the shortage of certain food stuffs. Hitherto it had deceived itself by imagining that the rising prices came entirely from profiteering and market manipulation. To the last moment the Asquith Government had delayed official interference. Now a Food Controller was proposed, his duties being vaguely named to include production and distribution. In August, two months before, a Committee had been appointed in response to public fears to inquire into the whole food question and to propose what remedies seemed advisable. Incidentally, it made its report seven months later, after the new Government had been forced to anticipate it, without its assistance, by several weeks. And the Food Controller idea was left untouched for two months to the consideration of the people. It was a habit of the Asquith Government.

In December, when the people changed leaders, nothing practical had been done. The Food Controller had not been named. A score of proposals had gone no further. Week after week the newspapers were left to urge their own particular hobbies, to resist that which did not meet their fancy. And day by day conditions were growing more desperate. When Lloyd George took the reins one of his first appointments was the Food Controller, his duties limited to food distribution and food consumption; and other officials followed for the great problem of production. No one man could handle all ends of the food question.

Almost before the new Premier had settled down to individual problems came the submarine menace to importations, and instantly everything else had to be dropped for the greater anxiety. Without delay he realized that in the farmer was the only hope. There might be discovered means of destroying the submarine; there might not. And the latter contingency had to be considered first. An appeal was made to the farmer to break every available acre, and power was given the authorities to commandeer for tillage idle land. Allotments were laid out all over England for the townspeople to work after hours. A large order for tractor ploughs was wired to America.

But the farmers had become disgusted with the lack of consideration shown them thus far. Their response was: "How can we break land without the help to do it"? And when most of the tractor ploughs were sunk on the way over it became more than a condition that could be met by appeal.

The Ministry of National Service, a special production of Lloyd George's brain in anticipation of such problems, went to work. It concentrated on furnishing the farmer with the help he needed. It invited every man who could handle a plough to give up his present work and spend the next six weeks on the land while yet the season's crops might be planted. It began to train women for work they had never anticipated in their wildest dreams.

The Army was combed. Eleven thousand farm-hands were lent from the units training in England.

Twenty-seven thousand were taken from the trenches and returned to the land, subject to twenty-four hours' recall. Camp commandants were ordered to let out their draft horses to the farmers at a dollar a day. Five thousand German prisoners were put at work. Of the 60,000 farm-hands whose Tribunal exemptions were up only 30,000 were asked for, and before they could respond their number was reduced to 10,610.

The Government spent two million dollars on farm machinery. In the shortage of tractor ploughs every one was commandeered and men sought to keep them at work in three shifts day and night.

The Cabinet took a peremptory hand in the disagreements between the War Office and the Board of Agriculture. "In this particular case," it said diplomatically, "we regard the production of food as more important even than sending men to the Army." That was the last word. And to back up its decision it formulated conditions to control the relationship of farmer and helper, of farmer and the public.

In establishing terms that would induce the utmost extension of land cultivation the Government was faced by two problems—the "plough-fright" of the farmer, and the reluctance of the labourer. To a Canadian it may seem strange that concessions should be necessary to prevail upon the farmer to break all the land he could work, but peculiar English conditions had made it seem more profitable for him to let his land go to grass. Back in the early eighties and nineties he had felt the keen suffering of land poverty, when the inadequacy of prices for grain made his work a loss. And now the unknown future was further blackened by an uncertainty of labour to enable him to profit from the capacity of the land put under cultivation. Unless he could be assured reasonable returns from his labour for a certain course of years, he would not be likely to invite a repetition of his insolvency of thirty years ago. Next, the protection of the farmer would be of little avail if conditions were made insufficiently attractive to draw the labour to him in steady supply.

Therefore the Government attempted in one stroke to overcome both obstacles. It established minimum prices for six years for wheat and oats, and minimum wages for the worker. Wheat, at the time this announcement was made, had reached $2.25 a bushel, and working roughly from this basis and considering the cost of production, the minimum price for 1917 was set at $1.78 per bushel, ranging down to $1.34 during the last three years of the period. Oats were to bring not less than 65 cents this year and 45 for the last years affected.

It must be remembered that the prices were *minimum* only. That is, there was nothing to prevent the farmer accepting whatever the market would give him above the scale. As I write wheat is quoted at $2.75 in England, and should the submarines continue, even as at the present, the price will advance much higher before the year is finished. At first glance it might seem an unwarranted protection, an unjustified drain on the country during its struggle for reconstruction and a world's markets in the early period of peace. But there is no more theoretical right to the Government to force the farmer to raise wheat than a tool maker to make shells. The latter has been forced, or practically forced, but common equity demanded that the country take the risk. And the nation must have wheat whatever the cost.

The matter of wages was equally important. No one in England with ambition went into farming before the war unless that was what he had been brought up to. The wages were only a few cents a day, and the life was miserable, as befitted the social scale to which the industry had been driven. A cowman had become the symbol of stupidity—because no one with thought would accept the pittance of reward for his labours. Under the rising prices of war times the farm-hand could not purchase the necessaries of existence on the old rates, and wages had to rise. The scarcity of help was another factor that forced the farmer to pay more. But when the Government saw the necessity of turning labour to the land by the hundreds of thousands it realized that something adequate in the way of wage must be assured. Accordingly the minimum wage for even the novice was set at $6.25 a week, which is not high when it is considered that the farm-hand keeps himself. That it is not too high is proved by the lack of protest from the farmers. In fact some are offering two dollars a week more, and even higher. The farmer's outlook on life has broadened with the new conditions and with the prospect that opens up to him in the future. The war has remade him.

One of the surprises of the war is the facility with which women learned the disagreeable, arduous tasks of the farm. And the farmers, after fighting female labour on principle as contrary to common sense and destined to deprive them of the men they preferred, are ready to declare their conversion. Six months ago 140,000 women were performing men's work on the farm, and the number has doubled since. Training farms have been set aside for them now, with free keep and training. After that they are placed on farms under female supervision, and paid $4.50 a week, without keep, uniforms found. That there is insufficient margin seems evident from the attempted justification of the Department that munition hostels have proved that their keep need cost no more than $3.75 a week. Of course the woman may take as much as she can induce her employer to pay, and with experience she has demonstrated her ability to earn the equal of the English man. Formerly women were not paid enough on the farm to keep them, in many cases, so that their volunteering was a sacrifice even of money. Under the new condition thousands of girls are leaving the kitchen and the factory to till the soil.

The introduction of Sunday labour is another feature of the war affecting the farmer. While England has never—at least of late years—observed the Sabbath as strictly as Canada, Sunday labour was not recognized as either necessary or desirable. The immediate necessity of spending every moment on the land could not, however, be denied during the early months of this year. All over London allotment workers were busiest on their only free day, and even an official appeal advocated uninterrupted ploughing. And several Bishops gave it their sanction. The farmer's week has become, therefore, a full seven days of work.

The exciting market conditions that have marked the progress of the war and its effect on the supply of food stuffs have brought the English farmer into personal touch as never before with the reason and justification of price levels. It has revealed to him his inexperience in marketing and the profit accruing from a more intimate knowledge of the conditions that affect prices. That inexperience has left him thus far the prey sometimes of the middleman's smartness, sometimes of his own greed. From the first he has insisted through his organizations that he be left to reap the utmost benefit from the relationship between supply and demand, ignoring the fact that much of the fluctuation of price has been due to the manipulations of the supply house from whom all incentive to bring about higher prices would be removed if the farmer were to pocket the extra profit. Undoubtedly the farmer's demand is justified, with certain restrictions, but it would be the public who would profit, not the farmer. Should the farmer, however, have been left to take full advantage of public panic and prearranged manipulation, the conditions of living in England would have been intolerable; for he alone has the final control of the supplies.

The joint efforts of the three hands through which the farmer's productions reached the public threatened such dire things, however, that the Government was forced to establish prices. The most interesting commodity thus affected was potatoes. There was a world shortage, and it must, or should, have been known that the deficiency would centre in England, since the past season's crop had been largely ruined. England was supplying more than her share to the armies, and importation was difficult and unprofitable. Yet no attempt had been made to curtail waste or limit consumption. Thousands of tons a week were even being shipped from the country to adjacent neutrals. The extent of stocks was made public suddenly, a trick of the wholesalers and of little profit to the farmer at the moment. In two days the price leaped from two cents a pound to six. Threat of Government action sent it back again equally swiftly. But the fact was not to be ignored that England was going to be short of its favourite food. The farmer began to see his opportunity, and for weeks he was receiving as high as three and a half cents a pound. Then the Government took a firm stand. At first it was considered sufficient to limit the retail price, but the retailer and wholesaler tried to force the farmer down to such a ridiculous price as a consequence that he refused to accept it. And so the entire gamut of selling was covered by the Government order. The farmer was to receive $45 a ton from the wholesaler, the wholesaler $52.50 from the retailer, who received in turn $70 from the consumer. The initial attempt to make the farmer accept $40 was reviewed in a couple of days and the price raised a pound. But as there was nothing to prevent the farmer selling direct to the retailer, or even to the consumer, thousands of tons reached the table at the legal price with more profit to the farmer.

To meet the inadequacy of supplies appeals were sent all over the country that the wealthy should eat subsitutes and leave potatoes to the poor. Hotels began to have potatoless days, and by April 1st, when the legal price was to increase, several clubs were serving no potatoes whatever. Whether this decrease in demand will make the farmer regret having held back his stocks until the higher price was obtainable is not evident at the time of writing.

Wheat, of course, travelled steadily upwards to heights unknown since the Crimean War. And the farmer reaped the profit. Milk advanced to twelve cents a quart, the farmer following its rise more closely than his other productions, until at that price it could not be handled by the dairies. And again the Government interfered. But the result of the interference was to drive the farmers from keeping dairy herds; and now a higher price is announced for next winter's supply in order to encourage the farmer to continue his herds.

One contingency of the war painful to the farmer and working with seeming injustice was the commandeering of supplies for the Army. At first this was done with little regard to market prices, and always at a lower level than was obtained by the farmer in the open market. The ignoring of prevailing prices was stopped, but commandeering at something below market scale, even though it necessarily selects certain farms and passes others by, is an attendant of war. What sympathy might have been given by the public was killed by the orgy of profiteering that struck the farmers in the cases of potatoes and milk—although precisely the same principle is considered good business in all other branches of business.

Lament as he may, the English farmer's position has not been an unenviable one. What makes his trials more poignant to him is the inability to utilize to their fullest extent the opportunities that lie at his hand. For every idle acre now is lost money. He may not be netting the tremendous profits of the ship-owner, but neither is he taking the risk. And he escapes both income and excess profits taxes. Indeed, he alone of the profiteers of the war is exempt from any enforced return to the country. Compared with his brothers in France he is extremely favoured. Across the channel the farmer is not exempt from military service, the work on the land being performed by women and children. The English farmer is forced to accept substitutes who do not substitute, but every bushel he produces nets him twice what it did before, and the Government has protected him against the risks of future years. No other industry has suffered so little, but no other industry was on such an unwarrantedly low level.

His new standing in England will affect more than himself. The Dominions will not profit so freely from his migration, for his opportunities will be greater and there will be millions more cultivated acres in England to justify his remaining at home. His standard of living will be raised, and his position in society will add a new dignity and self-confidence. It seems certain that the rights of landlords to idle acres will be drastically limited, and the farmer will be enabled to rise from the semi-serfdom of the renter to the independence of the owner of land on which his every effort will count to his own profit.

It can be said that the new English farmer of the future is the direct result of Mr. Asquith's procrastination in taking steps necessary to ensure reasonable production within the shores of England. Had protective measures been taken earlier the public would never have learned how dependent it was upon that which had been so long considered an unessential of English supremacy—the farmer and the farm.

Next month Mr. Amy will write about the working man and the war.

Labour and the War

By Lacey Amy (1877-1962)
Part III of 'England in Arms'
From *The Canadian Magazine*, July 1917.

No one is qualified to speak didactically concerning the relationship of English labour to the war. The medley of events that should form a reliable basis for deduction is apt to leave one more at sea in the selection of general terms for describing that relationship than would a less complete sum of information. The Labour Party of England has been perhaps as consistent and fair in its attitude as would be any other organization that held together for entirely different purposes two and a quarter million men, including many thousands —perhaps hundreds of thousands— who, from lack of opportunity or time or ambition, have not developed that equilibrium of reason which alone is competent to control the daily routine of one's existence to rational lines.

Labour has lent itself to the most uncompromisingly inimical deeds— deeds which if persisted in, would have accomplished that which the enemy can never effect. It has struck with seeming ruthlessness and disloyalty at the very foundations of the Empire. It has demanded that which to grant would have been to yield to the Germans. It has thrown down tools absolutely necessary to victory. It has declared for peace at any price. It has, in fact, permitted itself to run the entire gamut of treason at one time or another, in one locality or another.

But to judge from those black chapters in the history of an aggregation that must, like any other organization, be of motley sentiment in matters that do not immediately touch its *raison d'etre* would be as disastrous to authoritative conclusions as to estimate the calibre of the German from isolated acts. If one must deduce from individual incidents, there are those which stand out with unquestioned authority, with undoubted right to claim precedence in any consideration of the manner in which Labour in England has conducted itself towards the great struggle. Put to the vote, Labour has expressed itself in no ambiguous terms. It has given of its numbers in millions to the perils of the front. And its leaders have stood out almost en masse as examples of British patriotism and determination to overcome the enemies of the Empire.

The chapter of Labour treason is black, but it is only as black as a few of its unlicensed leaders whose hold on the imagination of the workingman has been their ladder to everything their perverted intelligence has considered worth while. Such men as Ramsay MacDonald and Phillip Snowden, types of the agitator who along with a certain cleverness and misused mentality, possess a keen appreciation of their sole claim to distinction, have never for a moment been Britons, even under the dire threat of the terrible war. And in their wake follow a number of lesser lights who are willing to emulate the worst of the "big" men they see as the simplest way of obtaining influence.

No consideration of the stand of Labour in England can arrive anywhere without first of all informing itself of the power of Labour before the war, as well as of its methods. Any numerically inferior political party that holds the balance of power in the nation's legislative chambers is certain to go astray in some vital particulars. However honest its legislative representatives, its unearned power will make it lust for more at the cost of fairness and unselfishness, will render unreliable its sense of proportion. And Labour was in that position in the British House before the war. Only a small fraction of the strength of the two parties in the House, it was yet of sufficient numbers to hold the weaker of the two in power, a condition which British law does not avoid even while fully conscious of its dangers. The Conservatives, easily the Government in point of numbers, were forced to remain in opposition. But only so long as the Liberals conceded to Labour its demands. The result was unavoidable without a change of Government; and the Labour Party was in a position to effect that at any moment it wished and as often as it wished with either party.

It might not be fair to say that Labour controlled Great Britain, but in theory it was so, and in fact, even as it is apparent to-day, it was nearly so. That Great Britain is what it is sums up the moderation and wisdom with which Labour must have yielded its almost unlimited power. The one outside restraining influence was that it knew it had little to expect from the party it has kept so long in opposition.

That accounts for the first stage in Labour's official connection with the war, as well as for most of the unfortunate acts of misjudgment it has indulged in since. Premier Asquith, perhaps the *cleverest* Prime Minister England has ever had, was not a free agent. Labour responded to the voluntary appeal for soldiers in a manner that did it credit, but when conscription was introduced it naturally, as the real party in power, refused to submit without question to that which it had not dictated. As has appeared since, the South Wales miners proved themselves the irreconcilables. Bluntly they refused to acknowledge conscription as applicable to them. And, since their number was so large and the stress too immediate and serious to risk coercion, Asquith could see nothing to it save submission. His political position did not depend upon it—at least not immediately— for by that time the Government was Coalition, but his impotence during the previous few years to fight Labour had put muscle into Labour's arm, and that muscle it was now exercising.

There was plausible ground for submission, since skilled labour was even then recognized as a necessity at home. Subsequent events have proven that the same principle should have been applied in a score of industries that did not fight to remain out of khaki. But both reason and subsequent events have more unquestionably proven that no body of men should be exempted as a body. The success of the miners put the idea into many other unions, and what had been granted to one could not be denied others of as great, or even greater, importance to the country. By November, 1916, no fewer than twenty-four unions had been exempted from conscription and Labour was creeping more and more beyond the encompassing arms of the recruiting officers. Only the substitution of Lloyd George for the weakening Asquith put an end to a condition that was growing more intolerable every day. And even the new Premier, as the latest attempt at combing out reveals, is unduly the slave of Labour, since he has agreed that no member of indispensable unions should be forced into the army save by the decision of a tribunal composed half of Labour.

Of these agreements of exemption for entire unions we have one sample. On September 28, 1916, Asquith had given out an undertaking that "skilled men (by which I mean men who from natural ability or training, or a combination of both, have special aptitude for particular and indispensable kinds of national work here at home) ought not to be recruited for general service". A month later the Amalgamated Society of Engineers demanded something specific for themselves, and Asquith granted it. The terms of that agreement are interesting as an example of failure by a war Prime Minister to reconcile union rights with the necessities of the nation. The first clause granted that the engineers, whenever they ceased to be fully employed should enroll—not as soldiers—as War Munitions Volunteers, "in accordance with arrangements now in existence under the new War Munitions Volunteer scheme". That is, an engineer—and he was but one of twenty-four unions similarly treated—should never under any condition be exposed to the trenches, even when his work ceased to be of a nature for which exemption was supposed to be granted. The second clause limited the application to men who were journeymen or apprentices prior to August 15, 1915, a year after the war started. Clause three stipulated that, when enrolled as Munition Volunteers, they be given exemption cards which prevented their removal without the consent of the War Office, "which will not be given without reference to the Ministry of Munitions and the executive of the man's union". In clause four it was inserted that statutory powers might be used as a last resort if the unions failed to supply sufficient skilled men for the Artificers' Corps in the Army or as Munitions Volunteers. And clause five assured the union that if it would furnish the names of its members now in the Army they would he transferred out of danger to the mechanical units.

These details are essential to an understanding of the powerful grip the unions have had on legislation. It was an unfortunate result of this immunity from service that many of the unions openly solicited membership on the ground that it carried with it such immunity. Scores of every-day incidents in factory life today might be added to prove Labour's power, but they are unnecessary here.

With such a record of irresistible strength it is no wonder that certain sections of Labour have shown instances of the seamy side of some of their members, even while it has in the mass demonstrated its loyalty. Strikes have been frequent, but fortunately of limited duration. Some of them—most, indeed, when Asquith was Prime Minister—were settled by the submission of the employers under pressure from the Government. Since Lloyd George took the reins the experience has changed. And once again Labour has shown its honesty by backing the new Premier as it never did the old.

The record of strikes during wartime will always stand to the discredit of Labour in England. Even Russia has been free from them in the nation's peril. But back of it all stands the spectre of Capital's treatment of it throughout the ages. For Capital in Great Britain has exhibited to its most disastrous extent the ridiculous distinctions of class that have done more than any other single thing to handicap England.

Just a word on this feature of English life. There never has been sympathy between Capital and Labour in England. The entire idea of the employer was to get all he could out of his workingmen at as little cost as possible. The workingman was but a cog in a wheel that was supposed to turn out dividends. As a human being he did not seem to count. No better proof of this calamitous relationship can be given than by mentioning the one insuperable obstacle to Labour contribution to the War Loan in hundreds of factories. "No," objected the workingman, "I won't contribute to the Loan, because I do not want the boss to know I'm saving money. He'll cut my wages if he does." I do not speak from hearsay; I personally faced such a refusal many a time.

So that it was no wonder Labour, feeling its power in the individual as well as in the organization, went to excess in spots.

The first menacing strike occurred most fortunately within the sphere of Lloyd George, although he was not then Prime Minister. In March, 1916, a serious strike was declared on the Clyde among the shipbuilders. It was the more serious in that it was engineered by the men themselves, directly against the leaders' wishes. Some half dozen shop stewards, who have since been declared to be in German pay, roused the men against the dilution of labour, and, catching them at an hysterical moment and after months of unbroken and unusual strain, combined them in a walk-out. As it happened, the Department immediately concerned was Lloyd George's. With a firm hand he promptly deported the six leaders and the strike broke up. It is interesting to follow the incident through. In January, 1917, one of the deportees appeared unexpectedly at the Labour Congress at Manchester—unexpected to the rank and file but not to the leaders, for the Government had given its consent that he should attend—and, wild-eyed and fervent, declared his intention of returning to Glasgow. The Congress cheered him, although the leaders tried to turn the tide. Kirkwood, the deportee, was as good as his word, although the Government, now under Lloyd George, immediately announced that he would be arrested. The Government, too, was as good as its word. And Kirkwood, finding the Government not now to be trifled with and his friends few, signed an undertaking to keep quiet. As that was all the Government had ever demanded of the deportees its victory was complete. Also the Labour Party, by staunchly refusing to support Kirkwood, proved its virtues.

Another threatened strike that would have disorganized the conduct of the war throughout the Allied countries was proposed by the South Wales Miners. This was their second interference with the course of the war. Both sides seem to have been to blame, the employers for the low level to which they had always ground the men, and the men for their unpatriotic demonstration at a moment when Italy and France, as well as England, were absolutely dependent upon English coal. The story is too long to tell here, but the South Wales miner, already having obtained various advances in wages since the beginning of the war, amounting to seventy per cent., was still unsatisfied. And the employers, although making higher dividends than ever before, thought they saw an opportunity of increasing them. While the miners demanded a fifteen per cent, increase, the owners asked for a ten per cent, decrease. Where the miners secured public sympathy was in agreeing to submit their case to an audit of the owners' books, which the owners refused. The crisis crowded eloser and closer, and at last the Government stepped in and took over the mines, immediately granting the miners their higher wage. This, too, was in Asquith's time.

There have been other strikes and threatened strikes by the dozen, but none of equal seriousness, largely because nipped in the bud. The different attitude adopted by Lloyd George has had its effect. Since he came into power strikes have been of short duration because the Government was not minded to parley to the nation's menace. The new Premier's metal was tried on the very day Asquith resigned. The boilermakers of Liverpool took advantage of administrative chaos to declare a strike. But Lloyd George took the Labour Party into his Cabinet by means of some of its strongest and most patriotic leaders, and thereafter he could not be accused of lack of sympathy. Hodge, the new Labor Minister, a Labor man himself, simply wired the boilermakers that no consideration whatever would be given their case unless they returned immediately to work. It was a new system, and it worked. The boilermakers returned. They realized what subsequent strikers are finding out, that the nation will not stand for strikes until the war is over. The Tyne engineers declared a strike towards the end of March, 1917, led by the shop stewards and opposed by the leaders. Once more the strikers were informed that their demands would not be listened to while they were idle, but this time they thought to make a real test and voted to remain out. When, however, a wire reached them from the Government warning them that if they did not return to work immediately drastic measures would be taken, they knew their stand was hopeless and took up their tools.

But the two great obstacles to the production necessary to victory came from the threatened breach of union rules demanded by conditions. One was the dilution of labor. The Clyde strike arose from the workingman's opposition to the introduction of women into domains that had always been his; and a hundred smaller strikes and a thousand disagreements have had their origin in the same cause. The Government could not but insist, however strong the opposition. Without women the war would never be won, for there are not enough men to do the fighting and the work. But even yet daily opposition arises from individual unions or branches of them. Labour has, however, sized the necessity as a body and has yielded to it.

The other handicap was the recognized scale of output by the English workman. It is almost incredible that any man would openly support the deliberate limitation of his output as a system vital to his well-being. The idea has sometimes been secretly preached in America. But in England it was a recognized union principle to "ca' canny". In that, too, the employers were largely to blame, for the wages they persisted in paying were unbelievably small. No workman could do good work on them; no workman could maintain his self-respect on such inadequate and miserly pay.

And along with the limitation of output came the attendant evils that assisted its development. Absenteeism was a habit. In part it was due to liquor, but there was nothing in his life to make a workingman desirous of limiting his potations to reasonable quantities. Every holiday—and the English year is full of them—was followed by two for recovery from the effects of the day's sport. In a few words, England was producing much less than half her capacity and had grown accustomed to it. That was why she was losing her grip on the world's markets. But half-production did not gibe with war necessities, and an alteration was demanded. To a great and surprising extent it has come about. Many a labourer has seen the necessity as well as the Government and has buckled down. To some extent liquor was put beyond his reach, by shortened hours of sale, by the closing of the more dangerous saloons, by an increase in prices, and by the anti-treating law. But some effect also was wielded by the hearty way in which the women assumed their share of production. They were not broken to limiting production as a principle, and factories have boomed for no other reason than that the men see that their very living after the war depends upon a demonstration of their capacity. Pride does the rest.

There are, of course, certain sections of the Labour Party which as a whole have opposed the war. The Socialists are divided, one group expressing its unalterable fidelity to the national cause, the other exhibiting only the worst side of Socialism. The Independent Labour Party is frankly for peace as a body, although a few of its leaders cannot agree to peace at any price. But these two disloyal sections count very little in the numerical strength of Labour and less in influence, despite the publicity given the peace meetings that are usually broken up by fellow unionists or soldiers.

It is in Labour's vote that it shows its soul. The Congress of 1916 supported Asquith's war policy by something less than four votes to one. In the Congress of 1917 the support for Lloyd George was more than five to one. When Lloyd George proposed to comb out the unskilled from the South Wales miners for the Army, thus daring much in the teeth of the most troublesome union, the union at first voted against the proposition and then rallied and supported it by three to two. And whenever a complete vote has been taken there is unmistakable evidence of the patriotism of Labour.

In its leaders Labour has been favourably represented. There is no hesitation there, no willingness to sacrifice the nation to union principles that held in peace time. With very few exceptions the chiefs of the organization are patriots. Much of their active co-operation has been induced by their incorporation into Government offices where they not only see the need of the times more clearly but are on their honour to cater to it. From the beginning, however, they have aided the authorities in bringing home to their fellows the demands of the fighting front. "Whatever is needed to win the war will be given," says the secretary of the General Federation of Trade Unions. J. H. Thomas, M.P., general secretary of the Railwaymen, one of the strongest unions, while watching the Government closely, is a staunch supporter of any measures that promise to win the war. The heads of the British Workers' National League condemn all labour disputes in war time. The British Socialist Party has repudiated enemy Socialists. Will Thorne, M.P., is a tireless advocate of aggressive war measures. Bent Tillett, whose influence over Labour has been frequently proved, visited the front early in the war and returned one of the best recruiting agents the country has had.

The effect of the war on Labour no man can foresee with accuracy. The longer the struggle continues the better the results for England and the workingman, so far as the establishment of desirable principles and methods are concerned. Much depends upon the attitude of the returned soldier—and where he will stand even he himself does not know. Should he settle down with the idea that he has completed his life's work and that hereafter the country should keep him, there will be years of unsettlement and disorganization. Should he resume his tools under the spur of years of military discipline, of widened outlook, of gratitude for peace, English Labour will carve a new groove for itself. There is talk in some unofficial corners of a great strike to come with peace, intended, it is said, to revive immediately the old methods and laxness. But against that will stand determinedly a nation .and many Labour leaders who see that only in grim hard work will England be able to hold her own in the world's reconstruction. Did Labour stop to think it would realize that anything it does to interfere with that great end will react upon itself.

The strike among the engineers engaged on munitions was not a Union affair. Indeed, it was strongly condemned by the leaders. It was organized entirely by the shop stewards, who had a secret union of their own, and was the result of the fear of youthful shirkers in control of the local unions that they would be taken from their jobs for service at the Front. Other strikes had to some extent the support of their immediate leaders, but there were conditions that mitigated the treason of downing tools when the Empire was at stake, although nothing could justify such an act. Thoughtful union leaders tremble lest Trade Unionism has dug its own grave, for, after all, it is the rank and file that make up the Union.

One thing is certain, that Capital and Labour will work on new levels, new understandings, new agreements.

Liquor and The War

By Lacey Amy
Part IV of, '*England in Arms*'
From *The Canadian Magazine*, August 1917.

PREJUDICE, in a study of the drink question in England is disastrous to conclusions that are either sound or safe in this time of war. The temperance "crank" is faced at the start by a great problem of expediency which concerns the co-operation of the very public he presumes himself to be considering. It is not merely a question of "reforming" a people against their will but of avoiding their antagonism at a time when even public carelessness and lack of active sympathy may be more disastrous to the Empire than the worst imaginable effects of the present extent of drinking alcoholic beverages in England. On the other hand, the noisy supporter of "liberty" has against him a volume of figures and unassailable records of the effects of liquor on the heart of the Empire that takes the ground from under his feet.

So tremendous is the problem, so extensive its side issues, that no magazine article can attempt more than a mere cursory consideration. Especially is this so in any presentation of the facts to Canadian readers, who have first of all to understand conditions in England before even reaching the general question of prohibition or abolition.

A concise review of the complications that overthrew instantly the stock arguments of both sides may be the best preparation for a calm consideration of the existing legislation touching on the consumption and manufacture of liquor. At this moment the immediate problem in England is the supply of food necessary to sustenance and strength, to which is added the corollary of the demand for man-power. Apart from the world's shortage, which would presuppose in countries the recognition of the wisdom of applying all food stuffs to their most complete uses, victory to the Empire depends upon the maintenance of the United Kingdom's share for the United Kingdom's people and armies. And that maintenance is almost entirely a matter of ocean tonnage, since eighty per cent, of the food of the United Kingdom is imported. The Government can reasonably depend upon a certain proportion only of the tonnage space of ocean vessels reaching English ports; and since the available tonnage is already insufficient it is most important that every inch of it should be of the greatest concentrated food value. It is for that purpose that the importation of luxuries has been prohibited, that our newspapers are reduced to the minimum size, that even complete foods like nuts and fruit have either been cut from the lists or limited.

Under this heading I quote figures that have been used in the public press and presented officially in the House without contradiction, so that their reliability is unchallenged, especially when the press and the House are against abolition. The beer production of the United Kingdom in 1914 was 36,000,000 barrels, with almost an equal amount of spirits—one and three-fifths barrels for every man, woman and child. In 1915 it fell to 34,500,000 barrels of beer alone, with the spirits almost the same, and during 1916 the beer was reduced another million. The materials used in 1914 (barley, hops, sugar, etc.), amounted to 2,100,000 tons for distilling and brewing, the former being one quarter of the whole. For the transportation of this material there would he required almost 1,200,000 *net* register tons of shipping (2,700,000 measurement tons), more than the capacity of ten boats of 5,000 tons size a week, or one hundred and ten boats continuously making five voyages a year—more boats than the Germans were able to sink during the first two months of submarine ruthlessness.

Taking last year, 1916, as an interesting example of the martial years: During that year there were a million and a quarter tons of barley turned into liquor, 305,176 tons of other grains, 67,578 tons of rice, maize and similar preparations, 134,000 tons of sugar, and 41,115 tons of molasses. All that in the third year of the war. What this vast quantity of food materials since the beginning of the war means in human sustenance is best explained by the estimate that it would make two billion two-pound loaves of bread and the sugar would support the entire army. And the ships required to transport it would have a total tonnage in the same period greater than the entire sinkings by the enemy up to the middle of 1917. At the end of 1916 there were still 1,800,000 tons of shipping in such employment.

Selecting sugar as the commodity of greatest stringency thus affected, the brewers have faced therein their strongest opposition, since the greater part of England has been on short sugar rations since early in 1916.

But there is other wastage attributed to the manufacture of liquor

100

in wartime. The expenditure by the United Kingdom in liquor during the war is estimated at more than two billion dollars, or sufficient to provide all the expenses of war for more than two months of the most expensive period. More than 30,000 acres were devoted last year to the growing of hops. Seventy-five hundred trains were required to haul the materials (and the train shortage is one of the problems of the war), and four million tons of coal were used in the breweries; and the Navy, the munition works, the dockyards, the Allies, and the people have suffered seriously during the winter from lack of coal. For the mining of this coal more than a whole brigade of able-bodied men are required; and the man-power represented in the breweries, the addition trains, the porterage, has never been estimated save in the form of being the equivalent of the entire nation standing idle a month and a half every year.

The drinking habits of the English affect the progress of the war in other ways. What is called absenteeism is the habit of the average workingman to holiday on days not legally granted him. The English working year is, to the Canadian, a bewildering series of customary and legal holidays. New Year's lasts for ten days in some sections in peace times, Christmas from three to five days, Easter from Thursday to Tuesday, Whitsun in some places a week, but always three days, and so on through a list unknown in number and scope to American experience. Great manufacturing firms stop work in mid-summer to enable their employees to spend a week of mirth and relaxation at Blackpool. And each legal holiday is rounded off by another one or two in recovery from the effects of the gaiety in which the working-man's holiday-making leads him to indulge. No fewer than five million hours were lost by absenteeism in one war year by Clyde firms, the average in one firm employing 1,500 hands being nine hours each man every week. Indeed, it was before the war customary in many localities and occupations to consider work accomplished on Mondays as so much to the good, and large manufacturers tell me even today that their average working week is four days. For this liquor was either responsible or a contributory cause. The condition was generally recognized and accepted as unavoidable—so much so that the improvement since the war began is taken as a matter for pride. Early in the war the figures concerning absenteeism were made public, but so startling and unendurable were they to English pride that Lloyd George almost sacrificed his political future in the public use of them. They constituted a fact that could not be contradicted, the effect of which on the vital industry of war-waking dare not be permitted to continue.

There is the other side, of course, but it will not be so readily understood in Canada as it is in England. The main contention of the brewers— supported by many influential newspapers and writers—is forced to concentrate on something more weighty than liberty of action. Wartime is independent of such arguments; liberty counts only when it does not threaten the State. It will come as a surprise to Canadians to know that the defence for the manufacture of beer is that it is *necessary*. It is seriously contended that hard workers *must* have their beer. Large advertisements repeat it ominously. Letters to the daily press insist on it. The soldier is wont to present his experience as clinching the argument. The working people are unable to contemplate abstention any more than the English man or woman of a different class would submit to prohibition of afternoon tea, which is considered as essential a meal as breakfast. It is a question of how far a national habit becomes a necessity. The very seriousness of the claim entitles it to more consideration than people accustomed to other ways might be inclined to give it.

The debate between the two parties to the question reached its keenest interest towards the end of 1916 when legislation was obviously necessary in view of the food and man-power needs. Availing themselves of the remarkable power of the English press, both bought space plentifully and presented their arguments for human digestion. On the one side was ranged a body of men among whom were many of England's greatest. The Strength of Britain Movement they called themselves. The composition of the organization added to its strength, for it was not made up of temperance fanatics or no prohibition advocates, but of men who normally took their glass but claimed to see in the exigencies of war sufficient grounds for prohibiting the manufacture of beer and spirits. On the other side were those to whom the liquor traffic meant wealth or a living. Even the brewers submitted to curtailment of production without serious opposition.

One day the Movement would give figures and draw deductions. The next day the opponents would criticize figures and deductions. It was fair forensic pleading until the anti-prohibitionists resorted to an unfortunate form of deception. A page of mild tolerance or frank support of beer drinking would be arranged in the same form and make-up as the Movement advertisements, and would be concluded with the words "it is part of the Strength of Britain", the last three words in a line by themselves in the same type as the same words in the Movement's advertisement. To the casual reader it seemed like concessions from the Movement. But the scheme was too un-English to be profitable in England.

The anti-prohibitionists claimed that the sugar for beer was entirely unfit for public consumption. The other side countered by reproducing an order from the Port of London authorities forbidding a large London caterer to remove from the docks a shipment of sugar consigned to him, because it was needed by the brewers. The yeast by-product of the beer was necessary, said the brewers. Look at Canada and Russia, replied the Movement. The trade was necessary, locally and for export. The answer was that its prohibition was necessary for the winning of the war, according to the Prime Minister. It was pointed out that from every ton of barley used for beer there was a large quantity of excellent cattle food upon which the milk of the nation depended. The statement was met by the counter one that the offals fed to cattle was infinitely less valuable than the whole barley. The demands of the army were emphasized, and on that the Movement was silent. The place of alcohol in munition making had to be admitted. The revenue from beer taxation was made much of, and was faced by the million and a half dollars a day paid by the public as its drink bill over and above the tax receipts by the Government. The brewers contended that tea and coffee occupied more space in the tonnage than the materials for beer; and that, too, the Movement ignored.

Two incidents embarrassing to the advocates of continued production occurred in the House, and England's sense of humour was tickled. The brewers had rashly contended that a given quantity of barley and sugar, etc., produced more than their weight in beer, a food product. Intended only for the consumption of the unthinking, it was brought up in the House. The Secretary concerned tartly asked where the extra food value came from. When the brewers ran a series of advertisements contending for beer as of real food value, the Secretary agreed with a questioner that if that were so then the imbiber should eliminate other food in order to come within the rationing orders of the Food Controller. That argument died suddenly.

It was a merry fight while it lasted, and the arguments were a mirror of the peculiar conditions existing in England. The odds were unquestionably with the prohibitionists, but, only because of the war. Under peace England would not have concerned itself to read or listen. But barley is food, and food is a big factor in the Englishman's life, in bulk and frequency. The movement against liquor was strengthened by several factors of sentimental effect. The King's abstinence for the duration of the war spread to thousands of wealthy and middle-class homes. Insisting purely as a matter of expediency in which the way had been shown by a beloved Sovereign, the strongest advocates of abolition were those who were known to have no tendency that way under normal conditions.

Lloyd George's well-known principles and opinions have produced an interesting experience. As has been mentioned before, his over-frank advocacy of prohibition in the early stages of the war almost cost him his highest place in English history. The public outcry at that time against his bluntness in supporting his opinions was so loud that the most fearless man in English public life was silenced. For two years he uttered not another word on the subject, and when he became Prime Minister he for several months permitted himself merely to hint at his feelings, confining expression to a connection between the material consumed in liquor and the submarine menace. Indeed, as Prime Minister, with an eagle-eyed opposition studying his every move to discountenance him, he realized the wisdom of leaving prohibition statements to his subordinates.

In this public outcry is that which brings to a thoughtful halt those who would, without pause, close the saloon doors and dismantle the breweries. As an initial caution to walk warily is the backing the manufacture of liquor has long had in England. When a great church draws a large part of its revenue from the traffic, when a considerable portion of the wealth of England is locked up in it, there is cause for consideration whether the ammunition is sufficient at the moment for making the attack. There is in England no sentiment against the brewer, the publican, the drinker. Rather, the nondrinker is an object of ridicule. Among the most influential men in England are the brewers, and the publican is a citizen of rank ex-officio. Bishops not only have money invested in breweries but preside over Associations that own public houses. The bar is not a place for a man to sidle into, and for women to avoid. Men and women enter one of the three or four entrances that feature the English saloon as a Canadian would enter a store to make a purchase. Since the selling hours were limited there is always a line-up at the doors before the time of opening. Young men take their girl friends in as to a Canadian ice-cream parlour, and women and men spend the evening therein as the great club of the common people. Before the doors, especially on Sundays, stand baby carriages and wee children awaiting the re-appearance of mother. In England and Wales there are 90,000 public houses.

The greatest surprise in England to the average Canadian is the unlimited patronage of the bars.

The result of this licence is a mental attitude that forms an essential feature in any fight for prohibition even in war time. In peace the prohibitionist has a hopeless vision.

Where the question of expediency enters is that, however convinced the ardent prohibitionist may be that the elimination of liquor would hasten the end of the war, he has first to consider whether the people would be with him. Failing their support there is the uncertainty of the effect of prohibitive measures. A nation convinced that it is doing no wrong is not going to see its pleasures cut off without dangerous protest. And the English workingman has a habit of expressing his displeasure in effective form. There is not the slightest doubt that thousands would prefer even to lose the war rather than to lose their beer; and the Government that attempted to introduce prohibition at this time would stare into a list of other conservation measures that might be enforced with the consent of the people, without attacking the workingman's entertainment. It is also feared by some prohibitionists that any attempt to enforce prohibition would meet with such opposition that the revolt would mean retrogression in any honest movement later towards that consummation.

The general attitude of the people is not uncertain. A vote to-day would overwhelmingly defeat suggested interference. Whether there would be open revolt or repudiation of loyal sentiments no one is in a position to say with complete authority. Judging from the munition strikes now on, the experiment would be dangerous. What is desirable in effect is not always what is possible or wisest at the moment.

It is considerations such as these which have handicapped the Governments of the United Kingdom since the first of the war. The wisdom or restriction was not associated in any way with decided predilection for prohibition. The early acts of Parliament forbidding treating and curtailing the hours of sale were intended to deal with a great waste in man-power more than in food. That they have done so to some extent is certain, but other influences have cropped up that have discounted their effectiveness. The higher wage has enabled the heavy drinker to indulge himself, and the more thrifty one to open his pocket. The effect of army life, too, has been to throw liquor into the way of those who had never before fallen seriously under its influence. The drinking among women has varied in the experience of different sections. In a general way the wife's allowance has provided her with resources for drinking previously denied her; and the missionaries of London say that conditions among them are terrible. On the other hand the report of the Control Board casts doubt on such an opinion. Some investigation which I have given the matter myself reveals the existence of more drinking at home, partly because of the shorter open hours, largely because there is money to purchase in greater quantities for organized orgies.

The official figures are so easy to misinterpret. The convictions for drunkenness in London and forty other cities and towns in Great Britain of a population exceeding 100,000 amounted in 1913 to 119,000 men and 40,000 women, in 1914 to 115,000 men and 41,000 women, in 1915 to 126,000 men and 38,000 women, and in 1916 to only 53,000 men and 24,000 women. That these figures are misleading may be gathered from the fact that the consumption of absolute alcohol decreased between the first and the last years by only twenty per cent. Of course several million men were out of the country in 1916, and the absence of relation between the number of convictions and the amount drunk is explained by the greater latitude allowed the drinker. The Home Office had issued an order—which was withdrawn in January of this year—that soldiers' wives were not to be charged for a first offence; and drunken soldiers are very leniently dealt with, while officers are disciplined only by the military courts. It is admitted by the magistrates that there is more drinking but fewer convictions.

At the same time it is due the soldier to say that very few are visibly drunk on the streets of London; and unfortunately the number of Overseas men, Australian and Canadian, has been greater than their proper proportion. This is explained partly by the eagerness of the

English to "entertain" the Colonial, partly by Canadian inexperience with English beers.

The early efforts of Lloyd George to effect prohibition having failed, and the anti-treating and short hours regulations having proved ineffective, the taxation on liquor was increased. But the increased wage of the munition maker rendered that move abortive, and a Liquor Control Board was appointed. The duty of this body was to control the interference of drunkenness with munition making, and for this purpose they had absolute power over the public houses of certain defined munition areas. The effects of the drastic measures it enforced were immediate. Some bars in dangerous districts were closed, the open hours of others limited, and model public houses were set up. The weekly average of convictions within their territories in six large cities showed a reduction of almost sixty per cent., and students of the figures found a direct connection between the open hours and the number of convictions. In England, up to the middle of February of this year, the Board closed eighty-five licensed premises in Great Britain. As the members of the Board are not prohibitionists there can be no criticism by the antis of their honesty in enforcing that which they consider necessary for the maintenance of the output of munitions. Sunday selling was forbidden, but mineral waters and soft drinks were permitted, the patronage under such conditions proving that the bar is more of a club than a welcome opportunity for dissipation, a fact emphasized by the Board in its report.

In August, 1916, the output of the brewers was restricted to 85 per cent. of the quantity produced during the previous year. On December 27th, a Defence of the Realm regulation permitted the naval or military authorities, or the Ministry of Munitions, to close altogether or curtail the hours of licensed premises. That this power was confined to an unproductive impotence is shown by the demand of the authorities at Aldershot, the great military camp, to close fifty per cent. of the surrounding public houses. The Licence Commissioners first consulted the brewers and then refused.

On January 3rd, 1917, when food shortage loomed in the near distance, it was promulgated that spirits should be reduced to thirty degrees under proof, the regulation not to apply to liquors bottled before June 6th, 1916. It was throughout this period, when further restrictions were certain, that was waged the newspaper advertisement debate, the Government standing—as it does in England during newspaper discussions—to see how the public stood before taking action.

On January 24th, the Food Controller, head of the new department called the Ministry of Food, founded but not peopled in the time of Asquith, announced that after a careful investigation of the resources available for food for the people he had come to the conclusion that the materials used in the manufacture of beer must be curtailed. After April 1st the output was to be further reduced to 70 per cent. of the output for the previous year. Thus the brewers had two full months to increase their output so that their licence for the coming year might be as liberal as possible. A corresponding restriction was applied to the release of wines and spirits from bond.

The effect of this legislation was that an output of 36,000,000 barrels before the war was reduced in two stages to 18,200,000. It would mean a reduction in the use of barley of 286,000 tons, 36,000 tons of sugar, and 16,500 tons of grits. Lord Devonport also pointed out that it would set free for the use of agriculturists a greater percentage of offals than was previously produced from brewers' grains. Whereas the brewers returned 25 per cent. of the barley as offals, the farmer would now have 40 per cent, after the other 60 had been made into flour.

Three weeks later it was decreed that no new contracts must be made for the delivery of malt to brewers nor must brewers make it for themselves. At this time it was shown that practically no spirits were being distilled except for explosives. The query as to why the 140,000,000 gallons then in stock was not drawn upon instead of using new materials was replied to in the House by the official statement that it would not pay, although that step would be taken if found necessary. Ten days later the manufacture of malt was entirely forbidden except with the consent of the Food Controller.

During these few weeks there had been much public discussion of the waste of food stuffs in the manufacture of beer, and the submarine menace was opening the eyes of the people to the seriousness of the shortage. The Government took notice of popular feeling by revising the regulation issued only a month before, to come into effect in another month. The output of beer was cut down to 10,000,000 barrels, thus saving 600,000 tons of food stuffs. Towards the end of March, the sinkings of merchant vessels having become alarming, the various restrictions seemed justified. Some attempt was made, both in England and France, to exempt French wines from the limitations, but the conditions did not admit of argument even on behalf of allied nations.

As the law now stands there are 367,000 tons of barley, 21,420 tons of grits, and 44,700 tons of sugar being utilized for the manufacture of beer. Whether it is possible to convince the public that much of that vast quantity of food can be better directed depends to a great extent on the future record of submarine sinkings. The demand for further reduction, and even for prohibition, is undoubtedly louder, although as yet not one of the powerful London papers has advocated the latter. It is a peculiarity of the standing of the English press that no such startling change could be effected without newspaper support.

For many months there has been a strong agitation for State purchase as the only feasible method of controlling the waste of food and the menace of drunkenness at such a time. The brewers resist it, probably because they know the temper of the Prime Minister, but they have lent themselves, with almost every other influence, to past restrictions and do not seriously oppose further steps in that direction. The most stubborn supporter of beer as a national stimulant is silenced by the Food Controller's statement that even the malt at present in stock would, if diverted to the manufacture of bread, supply the entire civilian population of Great Britain with the approved ration for eleven days.

State purchase has the official ear. It has the only public support of real weight. The fact that it was considered in 1915 and discarded as too heavy a financial burden has little effect on thought of to-day. That something must be done, and that prohibition would entail a risk the country does not wish to assume in midwar, seems to point to State purchase as the solution. And with it would go local option. Probably before this is read England will be expressing itself by local balloting upon a question which the greater part of Canada and the United States has already settled to its satisfaction.

The next article of this series is entitled "Education and the War."

Education and the War

By W. Lacey Amy
Part V of 'England in Arms'
From *The Canadian Magazine*, September 1917.

You may upset a nation's electoral system, revolutionize its labour principles, inaugurate a new standard of health—you may even alter its morals and reorganize its methods of trade—without a complete picture of national regeneration. But when the functions and direction of education are disturbed it is safe to conclude that the nation is stirred to its depths. And all these changes, even the last, the war has introduced into Great Britain.

Naturally such a creature of tradition has shifted its ground with a measure of apology, of denial even of that which it was in the very act of doing, but it has, nevertheless, accepted the lessons of experience and set about ordering its house. It is not the manner in which one works that counts, but the quantity one does. "If anyone doubted the value of our elementary schools," said Mr. H. A. L. Fisher, the new Minister of Education, in his memorable announcement of educational reform to the British House of Commons, "that doubt must have been dispelled by the experience of the war." And thereupon he proceeds to pull the system to pieces and to build from the ruins a new structure that will prepare the nation still more efficiently for the next war as well as for peace.

Great Britain, even before the war, was beginning to question her system of education as a complete equipment for modern commerce and competition. But with the first few months of the great struggle her gaze became focused on outstanding faults that were looming larger and larger with the ups and downs of the armies in Flanders. Something was wrong. The British soldier was as firm a bulwark as ever, but that which stood behind the perishable flesh and blood of the trenches was not fulfilling its part. German preparedness was demonstrating to a nation which had always had reason for pride that loyalty, a record for unconquerableness, selfconfidence, and determination were poor obstacles to the inventions of modern warfare. As Mr. Fisher put it: Great Britain was discovering that "the capital of this country is not merely cash and goods, but brains and body". "There is something in your d— board school education after all," a ship commander, glorying in the service of his men wrote him. But both Mr. Fisher and the House that listened knew the compliment was but an introduction to a practical expression of national dissatisfaction.

"One might have imagined," said the Minister, "that the war would have so occupied and exhausted the mind of the country as to leave room for no other thought. But it has had quite the opposite effect. Quite naturally, and as it seems to me quite rightly, this great calamity has directed attention to every circumstance which may bear upon our national strength and national welfare. It has exhibited the full range of our deficiency, and it has invited us to take stock of all the available agencies for their improvement." After such a confession of weakness, the most intolerant critic of the old educational system is content to await that firm stand for reform which is characteristic of the British nation when it sees its mistake.

The English educational system laboured under several disadvantages. First of all, in characteristic fashion, it was constructed like its castles— with an eye to its permanency. It is the British habit to build for all time. But if anything has been revealed by modern progress it is the superior value of adaptability to permanence.

It may seem treason to fly in the face of the hitherto much-quoted tribute of Sir Joshua Fitch to the English system of education. "The public provision for the education of the people of England is not the product of any theory or plan formulated beforehand by statesmen or philosophers; it has come into existence through a long course of experiments, compromises, traditions, successes, failures and religious controversies. . . . It has been affected . . . only to a small degree by legislation. The genius—or rather characteristic habit—of the English people is averse to the philosophical system, and is disposed to regard education, not as a science, but as a body of experiments to be discovered empirically and amended from time to time as occasion may require." But the new Minister of Education—and he is the first practical educationist in the forty-seven years of compulsory education who has filled the important post of Minister of Education—took issue, and the applause of the country proved that he shocked no sensitive susceptibilities in so doing. "More grant." he announced, "will be paid to an authority which believes in flesh and blood than an authority which puts its trust in bricks and mortar." And the House cheered as much at the suggestion of symbolism as at the reforms outlined.

The history of British educational legislation is so closely entangled with another of education's drags that it seems to demand attention here. In a country where Church and State have never been dissociated it was certain that the most influential institution should be demanded by the Church as its prerogative. And the struggle of the Church to maintain its hold has written a record of educational progress in Great Britain which is not a proud one.

The first state education came in 1832, when treasury grants were given in aid of elementary schools. Naturally at that time the early influences were religious rather than economic. It is in this condition, continuing through the decades since, that lay the strong foundation on which classicism stands, the dead languages being the door to theological learning of that period. Also, being controlled by the theologists. education, from the earliest days, was not conceived as a right to the masses, but as a privilege to those who might increase its power as well as be increased thereby. The baneful influence of the Church was evident in the long struggle that was fought out by old educationists concerning the basis of education. The Grammar School Act of 1840 attempted to improve elementary education without that subservience to its classical branches which had been considered its very essence, but the Church resisted the application of ancient endownments to schools not under its control. Up to the time of the Endowed Schools Act of 1869-1874 educational endowments, unless there was evidence to the contrary, were considered to imply instruction in the doctrines of the Church of England. In 1870 a form of compulsory education was introduced, but not until six years later did Disraeli make compulsion complete. In 1902, the time of the last real change in the educational system and the only one with evidences of permanency—in the light of later years—the pressure of the Established and Roman Catholic Churches for equal treatment with the voluntary and board schools brought about the abolition of the parochial school board and made county councils the local authorities. Two attempts to separate education from Church control were made, in 1906 and 1908, but both failed, the offer of the Government for the Church properties and endowments in the latter year not being considered sufficient.

The danger of Church control is its narrowness, its concern as much for its authority and influence as for the efficiency of its system. But times have changed. No flagrant deficiency, in Church or State, can long survive the opening eyes of the masses.

The third unfortunate influence on education in England is the snobbery of class. Even to-day there is the unexpressed theory that education, in its more advanced stages at least, is not for the common people. It can be taken for granted that every system in England is somewhat under the blot of the existing traditions of class distinctions. The war is overthrowing them in every phase of life, but the instincts are there, even in the proletariat itself. One has only to look at the general system of education to see it at its worst. Elementary education of the masses is conducted at what are called board schools. In a general way they correspond to the public schools of Canada. But they are handicapped by this essential difference—that they are not public schools in the sense which implies the patronage of the general public. In practice they are confined to the lower grades of society. To attend a board school, especially in the cities, is to be socially degraded.

Everyone who can afford it sends his children to private or public schools. The latter are in no sense public. Entrance is as firmly based on certain unalterable rules—and they have nothing to do with intellectual attainment—as is admission to the universities. A certain standard of wealth is evidenced by the ability to pay the fees demanded, and the boy's outfit is more precisely defined than the requirements of a girl in a ladies' college in Canada. Indeed, some social status is a necessity in many of the public schools of England, although the depletion of students resulting from the war is putting an end to that in the most effective manner.

Accordingly the system in public schools has followed a readily conceivable channel. Denoting in its initial stages a certain plane for the student, in wealth and often in society, the public school is conducted to further develop an estimate of life's responsibilities consistent with such an inception. In this I would not be misunderstood. There is nothing finer than the real English gentleman, but there is no Englishman, gentleman or not, whose outlook on life is not coloured by generations of training in exaggerated significances of social levels. The public school does not produce the snob so much as it produces those who appreciate class distinctions without permitting it to make them deliberately offensive. Its aim is to produce a "gentleman", that peculiar embodiment of virtues which, un-Canadian as it is in some of its opinions, is of a much finer clay than that which comes under the usual English designation, "gentleman".

To put it more affirmatively: The English public school, while it sends out a grand type of youth, handicaps him in the outside world by developing certain sides of him which are apt to neglect modern essentials and foreign opinions. It goes in for sports as a feature of the curriculum, a mark of the gentleman. It lays such stress on "sportsmanship" that war with the Hun, for instance, is a more perilous and costly operation than it need be. It adheres to certain lines of education in the face of the daily revelation of their inadequacy. It strengthens the disastrous conviction that tradition is the standard of excellence. It narrows even while it makes more indulgent. It builds up a fine fellow at the expense of his future in the world's competition. And yet the public school boy is imbued with so much of the best that is in the word British that, can he but forget some of his indirect training, he becomes the world-citizen who has built up the British Empire. When he fails there is nothing more intolerable. Remove the stain of the principle behind the public school, and the public school—barring one or two details—is beyond criticism.

An example of the parental attitude indirectly encouraged by the public school is afforded by a letter from a father recently read in public by a headmaster who was much impressed with the spirit of snobbery in its reds, but failed to sense it in its grays. "I wonder if I might ask your co-operation in regard to my son," it pleaded. "The boy's extraordinary liking for what I regard as the most repulsive branch of natural history—newts, beetles, and insects—is a source of much disappointment to his mother and me. Can you, either directly or indirectly, turn his mind to a higher and more refined branch of the subject—birds, trees, flowers I cannot help feeling that the tendency of the present study is degrading." It was the wail of a parent who was frank enough to acknowledge that public school as the propagation bed for caste education.

Public schools—there are 110 of them, with 35,000 students— are, of course, not officially recognized, although thirty-four of them receive grants and thirty-six are inspected.

In their upper grades they come under the general educational classification of secondary schools. And it is officially and popularly admitted that in secondary school education Great Britain has failed dismally, not alone in the snobbery it is inclined to encourage, but in the low educational standing of its teachers. Mr. Fisher declares that, in no other country is there such a proportion of secondary school teachers without a university degree. This is largely due to the small salaries paid. There are, it is well known, a comparatively small number of public schools whose standing cannot be questioned, but being out of Government control the majority have developed methods and standards of efficiency not conducive of the best results.

The secondary schools, whether official or private, failed, too, because of the multiplicity and lack of uniformity in their examinations. There are more than a hundred examinations demanded by the different callings and professions for which education directly prepares a boy. In every way there was discouragement for the lad forced to consider advanced education as a means to a livelihood. Thus there are three times as many pupils between the ages of fourteen and eighteen receiving systematized education in France as in England, and in Prussia six times as many.

In the universities conditions were not so bad, but still unsatisfactory. England has taken to itself great credit for the remarkable response of its universities to the call to arms. It is a fact that the great Universities of Oxford and Cambridge are almost empty, their examination rooms given over as hospitals, their laboratories to the inventions of war. But if the higher development of a nation's education does not breed patriots sad indeed is the lot of that nation. If education does not teach the true place of loyalty to one's country it has missed its greatest mental stimulation. It is to its universities—to its more intelligent classes—that any country must look for its salvation.

But the older universities of England had fallen into the national habit of conservatism, of settled lines of learning too slow to adapt themselves to the requirements of modern progress. This was especially evident in the prominence of classics at the expense of science and moderns, and what has come to be called the humanities. Based on the past, on the English reluctance to change, young men entirely unsuited for classical education, others to whom such training could be of too little value to merit its grind and time, were forced to devote themselves to Greek and Latin, when any modern language would have assisted materially in fitting them for the struggle of life ahead. And science was comparatively neglected. This light attention to science has exacted its penalty during these grim days. While the German was directing his perverted, but well-trained, mind to the production of the engines of war, Great Britain was forced to rely for counter-attack and protection upon those acute individual brains which have been the foundation of Britain's position in science, including its medical branch. Until the misdirected brains of the country could be switched from that form of development which tended only to the effective in oratory and literature, in abstruse dissertation and "intellectualism", the interests of the warring nation were subject to the attainments of those who had rebelled against a standard mould for the Englishman.

To be sure there had often struggled to the light rebellion against an unworthy appraisal of science, but the disadvantages of such a campaign are that its backers are obviously revolutionists, and their uncultivated weapon of publicity is dull compared with that wielded by those whose accomplishments are verbal, not practical. In 1889 the Technical Instruction Act supported technical or manual instruction, and a Department of Science and Art promised good results. But the Board of Education Act of ten years later swallowed up the new Department. And science became a study without direct usefulness, since it was insufficiently developed to adapt it to the needs of industry. Through mal-nutrition, too, even when it was productive it failed to meet the educated Englishman's demand for intellectual stimulus. And in English industrial life there was small reward for the scientist, a good works chemist before the war receiving a paltry six hundred dollars.

But protest and warning were coming from many sides. A number of new universities—Leeds, Manchester, Liverpool, and latterly, Bristol—had sprung up to cater to the crying need for a more practical education. Even Oxford was looking about for some plan of organized training in science that might be accepted as in conformity with its high standards. The universities were pricked into introspection by the clamour of the large industries that faced the competition of the outside world. Reverent as these industrial firms were towards the English university—their heads were usually university educated — they were the immediate sufferers from its inherent weaknesses. The head of one of the largest ship-building firms declared the other day that he preferred the university man in his works, but "when I go up to Oxford to look round I do not pick the fellow who has been first in Greek and first in History, but the fellow who would have been first if he had worked". It was a subtle pronouncement against the final aim of Oxford education, while applauding its general influence. He wanted the man with the Oxford brain, but not with the Oxford honours—might I say, ideals.

Several organizations were at work to introduce remedies. The Educational Reform Council intelligently attacked the administration. The Association of Directors and Secretaries for Education urged a number of reforms for continuation schools, pointing out the advantages of compulsory education for a limited number of hours a week for young people between fourteen and eighteen, whether in employment or not. The Oxford Association for the Improvement of National Education, the Departmental Committee on Juvenile Education, and the London Education Committee were striving for improvement.

But the most effective spur to reform came from the Workers' Educational Association. Mr. Fisher admitted that "our popular system of education is popular in one sense only". He saw that the schools of the people had not behind them the support of the working classes. The activity of opposition from the working classes came as a war result. Higher wages were bringing higher aims, a clearer perception of the possibilities of improved status. The workingman was ceasing to accept the doctrine that higher education should be reserved for the upper classes. And the Workers' Educational Association represented this movement, one of the most important, Mr. Fisher admitted, for the promotion of higher education among the workers. It ridiculed as entirely inadequate the eight hours a week suggested by the Departmental Committee, claiming that the hours of labour should be limited and the hours of education the real consideration.

The small salaries for teachers was an active issue even before the war, but with the increased cost of living and the growing demand for reformed education the teachers took a firm stand. In London they even went on strike against the miserly pittance allowed them as a war bonus.

The scale of salary of the English teacher reads like the record of Quebec Province a few years ago. In England and Wales there are 160,000 teachers, of whom 60,000 are uncertificated and 40,000 without training college experience; and almost none of them have university education.

Five certificated masters—two of them head-masters—and 219 certificated mistresses received less than $250 a year, twenty thousand (certificated) less than $375. A headmaster, after thirty years, had improved his pay from $435 to $480, another in forty years from $350 to $475. In one school in a large English county nine teachers (all in the school) receive less than the caretaker. The average salary for a certificated head-master is $880. for a certificated assistant $645. and for an uncertificated teacher $340. And women receive only two-thirds those amounts. In many counties the maximum salary for a certain grade of head-master is $15 a week; and the average salary for an uncertificated assistant is $325 for men and $280 for women. Yet the war bonus, with food one hundred per cent. higher, was sometimes as low as twenty cents a week.

Into conditions like these there was projected the first educationist to hold the Ministerial position; and in his choice Lloyd George made one of his many demonstrations of irreverence for tradition. Mr. Fisher knew the state of affairs from practical experience. Better still, he was uninfluenced by political or personal considerations. Starting with what he knew himself, he sought only what affected education. And he found it out. The result is educational reform that would never have come from the most honest politician such as those who have hitherto invariably filled the Cabinet positions.

Elementary education he first stroked, then admitted its deficiencies by granting an additional $17,000,000, chiefly as teachers' salaries. "An embittered teacher is a social danger," he declared. And the extra money is to be allotted by inverse ratio to the wealth of the district.

Secondary schools, "which are the key of the situation," are favoured with an extra two million dollars, the principal objects being higher salaries, more teachers, and encouragement for advanced courses. A strenuous effort is to be made, too, to drive out the caste system, so that "the son of the manufacturer, the son of the foreman, and the son of the workman should be educated side by side". Five years ago such a principle would have been killed at birth. For this purpose well-to-do parents are to pay for their children, while the Government comes to the assistance of the poor. The multiplicity of examinations is to be modified, although already a concerted attack has been made by narrow head-masters of some of the smaller private and public schools, who fear that candidates from uncontrolled schools might be discriminated against. This simplification of examination has been placed in the hands of a committee of eighteen, composed equally of elementary and higher education representatives.

A pension scheme for teachers is proposed.

Little has been done with the university system as yet, although action promises in the not distant future. Probably the Minister considered that he was undertaking a sufficiently large proposition for the present in reorganizing the less advanced forms of education. His tendencies with regard to the universities were expressed in a demand for "ample provision for the prosecution of free and independent post-graduate courses, and also for scholarships in science, technology, and modern languages". His attack on tradition consisted of a desire "that every child in this country should receive the form of education most adapted to fashion its qualities for the highest uses". He contended, too, for greater unity in the universities.

Without the war education in England would have proceeded along the old lines until the dire straits of inability to compete forced a change. While the record in England of the years immediately preceding the war showed a waning commerce in the markets of the world, only the very fight for existence revealed to the nation some of its weaknesses. To be forced for two years and a half to its limit merely to meet the war inventions of the enemy, without freedom to develop its own originality, has been gall and wormwood to the Briton. To look about him and see the ordinary conveniences of life missing because their supply had crept into the hands of practical Germany while England was advancing eagerly in philosophical and philological directions has opened the eyes of the nation to something lacking.

Therefore, when the new Minister proposed a drastic alteration in the very foundations of national life, instead of the customary outcry from the admirers and convention, Mr. Fisher is met with eager support. Education in England is being democratized, as is everything else. And therein lies the future of the Empire.

Part VI of 'England in Arms'
From *The Canadian Magazine*, October 1917.

BRITAIN, the free! Britain, the democratic monarchy! Britain, the mistress of the seas! Britain, the unconquerable!

They were sweet-sounding tributes whose title and warranty were never honestly questioned in time of peace. And the British nation had so incorporated them into its creed that nothing within the range of the most imaginative pessimist had for generations cast doubt on their eternal appropriateness. Through one war Britain had struggled with but the superfluity of her energy. Through centuries of peace the world had bowed to Britain's well-deserved reputation.

And then came war—war of the kind that recognizes no reputations, that develops along the ordinary channels of guns and strategy and men. And Britain was forced to revise her creed.

In that very revision came the real struggle. Britain, the free, had to reconstruct the meaning of the word. Britain, the democratic monarchy, had to acknowledge that democracy involved co-operative reality as a prime necessity for the maintenance of Britain as mistress of the seas. Britain ceased to be free. That was the bitter pill.

And yet Britain passed from freedom to bondage only in the interpretation of those who count nothing to a nation in its extremity. Bondage laid aside its ungrateful mask and became union, a great patriotic rally for the dominion of freedom. "United stand" was never so vividly demonstrated on the western side of the Atlantic. Freedom assumed its true meaning: the unassailable right to personal liberty so long as it does not infringe on the well-being of the state. Russia has tried the other kind of freedom for a few disastrous months and given the lie forever to the dreams of Socialism.

Born, bottled and bred on the freedom of the citizen, Britain entered the war as a Crusader. That first hundred thousand passed to France but as the vanguard of the millions that were clamouring to express their loyalty by force of arms against the enemy. The millions trooped to the recruiting offices, turning their backs on their occupations, their businesses, their comfort, their families. Voluntarism was to prove itself against every test. And for six or eight months it seemed to be succeeding. Faster than they could be trained and armed patriots rallied to the principles on trial. Great Britain was almost satisfied—the public part of it.

But there were military, and even political, experts who were not so credulous. Lord Kitchener had an inkling of what faced the nation. The Cabinet, shamed by its own unpreparedness, trembled. It handed over to the lion of the nation the task of affording voluntarism its greatest opportunity. What Lord Kitchener could not accomplish in the call to arms was beyond the power of any man in Great Britain. And Lord Kitchener's millions are a tribute to him and to his country.

But still the sweeping spectacle of Germany's might in those early months loomed high above Great Britain's show of resistance. Kitchener appealed as only he could. Posters stared where bills never dared appear before. Huge red arrows on every London street pointed the way to the recruiting stations. The King beckoned. Women urged and cajoled. The newspapers filled their front pages with petitions to the people. Appeals turned to warnings, then to threats. And the people thought they were hurrying. They saw the long lines before the recruiting booths, the long trains leaving for the front, the vacancies at home. But the authorities knew that longer lines must form, longer trains start, more homes be manless. For Germany was still near Paris, was still threatening Calais; and Mesopotamia, Egypt, Gallipoli, Greece were clamouring for fresh aggressive battle-fronts.

The Derby scheme was introduced.

It was in this Great Britain received its first taste of compulsion. The pill was sugar-coated at first. It was not a remedy, but a test. Every young man of military age was asked to report to the nearest recruiting station, not for service at the front, but for the compilation of a national register of fighting power. The sugar coating was very thin. The labour unions saw through it the first day. The entire country understood without accusing the Cabinet of falsehood in its declaration of intentions. But Great Britain was patriotic. It was also impressed with the promise that certain favours would be accorded those who attested should necessity for conscription arise. In millions the young men signed their names and ages and answered intimate questions. Lord Derby became recruiting agent extraordinary.

It was because the scheme was put forward as his and superintended personally by him that what obloquy attaches to subsequent events clings unjustly to his name. Lord Derby carried through the idea. Mr. Asquith perverted its expressed aim. The men who walked the streets with the khaki arm-badge as an evidence of their willingness to fight upon necessity were called upon before many months to make good.

Conscription killed its reputation only by its name. Conscription meant force, and personal liberty was the Englishman's religion. But Great Britain was strong behind the principle. Organizations sprang up in opposition, of course. There were the so-called pacifists whose hankering for publicity drowns every atom of their common-sense and reason. There were foreign outlaws seeking asylum in England, where they had fled to escape military rule and other pursuing evils. There were Socialists whose only tangible creed is resistance to authority. And there were cowards. The noise they all made in chorus was deafening. Those who accepted compulsion did so in silence; it was one of their virtues. Those who opposed it howled. And Asquith, impressed a little with his own breach of faith, and fully seized of the fate of his party in the event of an election, made every concession that could be made with any appearance of fairness and honesty. A Coalition Government was the first necessity. It was at that time indisputable that the party which attempted to enforce conscription might be on the road to hari-kari. And both parties in the new Cabinet lent themselves with remarkable unanimity to concessions. There were elections coming some day.

Ministers of the Gospel were exempted from service, some attempt at control being exercised by the stipulation that the sect must be recognized. There are enough religions in England to reform the universe in this generation—or wreck it. And with exaggerated British respect for conscience conscientious objectors were, freed with the Government's blessing.

The ministers presented only a small difficulty. But, since a man's conscience is a more private possession than his garters, there was none on this earth to decide with authority whether the conscience was for temporary use or was of that unfortunate stripe that becomes a habit, like drink, or cigarettes. Over the conscientious objector more strife has arisen than had he been forced to assume his share of national defence—his nation, his safeguard against coercion of conscience. His exemption was a political dodge, not British fair play. That is proved by the refusal of the House to deprive him of the vote he will not assist in making valuable.

And to prevent the conscription of others whose claims to

exemption might be as real if not as spiritual, local tribunals were set up to pass judgment.

Two conspicuously egregious follies have characterized the conduct of the Government in securing the men for the front. One is the brief for these tribunals, the other the recent efforts of the authorities to squirm around the question of trade exemptions. And of the two the refusal farce is the most complete exhibition of official folly.

The idea at the back of this consideration for special claims was beyond criticism. There must be thousands of cases where compulsion would work unpardonable injustice and disaster. Local tribunals seemed to offer the most available court and the least expensive. But the good judgment of such bodies could not have been considered. These tribunals were made up of local representatives of all classes. There were titled men, country squires, merchants, and labourers. Theoretically there was no favouritism in the personnel. However, it developed that every class of citizen had his advocate on the bench. And that was about all it did mean. Every claimant was personally known to one or all of his judges. The merchant resisted the conscription of his customers, the manufacturer of his employees, the workman of his fellow workmen, the farmer of his hands. Many of the applicants were in debt to one or more of the judges, and to send them to the trenches meant practically the cancellation of the debts. The tribunals as a body were prejudiced at the start against a duty that meant interfering with the business of the community. Indeed, many of them frankly contended that their chief duty was to protect local industry. The employees of members of the tribunals came before them and pleaded their cases, and while the employer usually retired for the decision, he knew he could trust his fellows as they would trust him when their turns came. Sometimes the members themselves were applicants for exemption. If it was an agricultural district, a farmer's helper was certain of favourable consideration. If it was a manufacturing town manufacturing became a national necessity. The applicant who had not a keen supporter on tribunal was rare.

Of course, the War Office attempted to exercise some restraint on decisions. The military representative might appeal, but if he succeeded the tribunal was likely to go on strike in protest. When Sir William Robertson was clamouring for more men there were tribunals who "downed tools" for a month at a time; and all that time the cases of hundreds of men hung fire.

Many of the exemptions were laughable, had they not been so serious. No occupation or profession escaped the leniency of these personal friends in the seats of the mighty. Pugilists, professional sportsmen, entertainers, labouring men whose only concern was to make enough to spend it in the pubs; clerks, workmen engaged on luxuries, men with nothing more to back their claims than a ready smile, were freely exempted. From hundreds of applicants for exemption only one or two would be turned down. A man would be exempted because his brothers were at the front, although he and his brothers had no financial or business connection; and lengthy eulogies would be showered on him for his family's patriotism. Weeping mothers and importunate fathers drew answering tears—and exemption for their boys. Even in July of this year a father secured exemption for six of his seven sons and one assistant, the other son refusing to share the family shame. There is even evidence that the members of a certain secret society were favoured.

Sometimes, aware of the weakness of their conduct, the tribunals retired into privacy to consider the claims before them.

It was a riot of favouritism, of blindness to the needs of the army, of selfishness. But the tribunals were no worse than the Government—not nearly so bad. Premier Asquith thought to lay the foundation to future political power, as well as to allay organized opposition to conscription, by exempting the members of twenty-eight unions. To give face to the act the trades were declared as essential to the war, but others, obviously more closely connected with the struggle, were ignored. And no restrictions were laid on this exemption through certificated occupations. If a man were a member of the Amalgamated Society of Engineers—even if he were making nothing remotely connected with warfare—he was exempted from service. The unions thus favoured openly advertised for members on the ground that membership meant exemption. Millions of young men flocked to the munition factories and other "essential" trades, were forced to join the unions, and were immediately exempt. It did not matter that their work a week ago was clerking, or following the races, or systematic loafing. An engineer was simply a member of the union and therefore immune from military service.

But the Government did not stop there. It added thousands of single young men to its departmental staffs and refused to release them for female or more aged substitutes. As with the unions, the fact that an able-bodied young man was performing some trivial duty in a Government office was his guarantee against khaki. More, the departments reached out and laid a fondling hand on hundreds of pugilists, and football players, and sportsmen, put them in khaki, and kept them in England, where they were permitted to fight (with their fists), or kick a football, for the honour of the unit with which they were connected. And each department head was his own tribunal.

Of course, there were departments, like the Postal, with a finer record, but all the attempts of the House to enforce respect for their country and its danger failed of complete satisfaction.

The Government defeated its own regulation in ways more open to criticism. Tribunals were ordered by department heads to exempt certain applicants without giving even a reason except that they were necessary to the country. They took men whose applications had been refused and placed them in easy Government positions. They opened their doors to the sons of friends without any qualification save their pull.

So glaring were these inconsistencies that even the tribunals sometimes went on strike against them. While married men approaching the age limit, with large families for the country to keep, classed in the lowest medical category open to the army, and owning large businesses which would be forced to close without their heads— while these men were heartily raked into the army hundreds of thousands of young, single, A1 men were posing as indispensables at a job they had picked up. It was even the case that Government factories were engaging these young men in the place of the older, married men while the tribunals were sitting on their cases.

Some of the newspapers took the matter up, especially the Northcliffe Press. Such a cry was raised in the House that certain departments were forced to release a few of these youthful slackers. But every month the fight has to be revived. Most of these young men loudly declare their inability to follow their inclinations, but they stand up under the restrictions with admirable fortitude and cheerfulness.

Not long after the start of the war Lloyd George's personal wishes on the matter were demonstrated in his contentions for dilution of labour, a task for which he was set apart by his leader. It is one of his greatest accomplishments that he was able to secure the consent of the labour unions, even at the payment of exemption. Women were introduced, and to-day they are entering factory shops where none but man ever worked before. The relief it gave to a situation whose seriousness will not be told until after the war was more immediate than even its most optimistic supporters expected. Indeed, the effectiveness of female labour, its versatility, its energy and trustworthiness, are partially the cause of the strikes that disgraced England during early May. The English workingman is having it brought home to him that his future is one of real work—with real pay—for the women have, in many instances within my personal knowledge, exceeded after a couple of weeks the output of the men who have been specializing on such work for years.

Dilution freed hundreds of thousands of men for the fighting line. And several minor measures affected the same result directly or indirectly. For instance, the jury system was suspended in some cases.

But against such saving of labour and freeing of men stands the multiplicity of officials. Work that might more honestly be done by boys and girls is in charge of uniformed officers and privates. A private firm would be scandalized by the duplication of work and inspection. It demands the services of three officials to measure the floor of a Government office to determine what to pay the scrub-woman. The streets of London are full of khaki-clad officials, exempt from fighting, but performing nothing that is beyond the capacity of boys or girls. And for some unadvertised reason certain men, like actors, are permitted to don khaki and continue their usual occupations.

Winston Churchill has stated in the House that there were three and a half men behind the lines for every one in the trenches. And in this Canadian military service, in London or France, is said to be little better.

When Lloyd George rode to power on a platform of aggressiveness, he organized immediately the National Service Department. It was a fine scheme, under an experienced business man and backed by a thoroughly roused public. It opened a whirlwind campaign of publicity that carried the nation off its feet. It called for a half million men hitherto exempt from age or physical condition or otherwise, as substitutes for ablebodied workmen in essential occupations. Sir William Robertson had publicly demanded a half million more men by July lst. Hundreds of thousands responded—and but one from every hundred was placed. As a department fiasco National Service stands alone. It died an unnatural death of violence at the hands of a disgusted people whose ardour has been cooled by this one act of official folly.

Then came the persistent necessity for something of real productive value. The men had to be secured. Thousands might have been combed out of the Government offices, but out in the munition factories were many times the needed number without a claim to exemption except the technical one of membership in specified unions. They were not essential to the output, because it had been proved that women could do better than many of them, and men graded B3 and C3 as well, and those who had gone into the factories since the war were openly exulting in their cleverness in thus escaping service.

There was encouragement to the Government to take them, because the union officials, finding their authority scorned by this huge new membership, longed for a way to free the organization of them. So the Cabinet announced a new dilution bill whereby those under thirty-one might be taken for the army. But the new union members defeated the measure in a simple manner. Without the acknowledged backing of one union official they organized a strike under their shop stewards. It is history that the Government at first counselled, then threatened, and finally yielded, as everyone knew it would. Politics was never more in the centre of the stage than to-day, with the Liberal party split into two factions and the Unionists watching their opportunity. (And yet coalition has been the salvation of the country.)

Since then the policy of the authorities has been one of unmitigated submission to a force they fear more than seems to a Canadian to be warranted. And to save its official face, as well as to introduce some sense of loyalty into the young shirkers in munition factories who are watching every official move, no public mention of the cowardliness and disloyalty of these young men was breathed in the consideration of the recognized labour unrest until six weeks after the strike was over. Then a couple of indignant members arose in the House and told the truth that was already known to everyone in touch with conditions in the factories.

Defeated once more in its efforts to raise the new army where the opportunities were greatest, the Government turned to other sources. The original minimum age had already been reduced, first to eighteen years and seven months, then to eighteen. Towards the middle of 1917 the other end of the age scale was tackled and men up to fifty were appealed for. To give the move some appearance of justice, it was announced that these older men would probably be required only for substitution, but in case they were needed at the Front notice would be given. But there was no exemption loophole provided. The tribunal folly was eliminated. Also it had been long suspected that fraudulent exemption on the alleged ground of physical unfitness was rife, and the men thus freed were ordered for re-examination. In one district it was discovered that one in every four exemptions was dishonest. Legal action was taken against dishonest medical examiners. As was suspected, the numbers of seemingly strong men wearing the badge of discharged soldiers were large enough to merit investigation. These, too, were ordered up for re-examination.

It was obvious that the Government was attempting to solve the problem by following the smoothest channel. The older men with expensive families for the country, the discharged and unfit— everyone who was not organized for opposition—was on the way to service, while millions of the very youths for military life were flaunting their immunity. Whereupon the discharged soldiers organized. First of all there was a spontaneous and natural protest against forcing re-examination on the obviously unfit, on the nervous wrecks.

And there the Government bowed to popular opinion. And when the case of the discharged soldiers was re-considered a compromise was made exempting those who had already served overseas, even though they had once again been passed by the doctors. But still the young men in the munition factories calmly issued their demands on threat of strike or decreased production.

Other unions proved their loyalty. There were demands from some of them to clean out their own young men. The South Wales miners, whose record of loyalty follows a fluctuating line, spoke through one of their representatives in the House. They held indignation meetings, at which they called upon the Government to take the 205,000 unmarried miners under the age of thirty-one.

At the same time London was swarming with aliens, subjects of allied countries or of none, who were replacing Englishmen in their jobs. It was estimated that in England were 200,000 friendly foreigners of military age. When the spectacle became unbearable and the public anger dangerous, legislation was introduced to force them into the armies of this or their own countries. Of course, the so-called Pacifists and those others whose only meeting-ground is their pro-Germanism, fought in the House of Commons to exempt these people; but the feeling of the House was overwhelmingly against them.

It was at this time was held the notorious Leeds Convention, in early June, an aggregation of Labour and Socialist anti-war, peace-at-any-price advocates who posed as representatives of British labour. It has been estimated that thirty-three per cent. of the delegates were Russian Jews, thirty per cent. conscientious objectors, and twelve per cent. acknowledged pacifists. As their object was solely to end the war to save their own skins or Germany's they received scant respect from the country. The experiences of Ramsay Macdonald and his friend Jowett will have done more than all the thousands of lectures and mobbings they have received to show them that there is a limit to human patience.

That is where the man-power problem rests to-day. What will be the solution is not at the moment apparent. Some say that the Government prefers to struggle along with what it has until the millions of the United States are available. At any rate, it seems certain that the present Government will not coerce the shirkers who have defeated it so easily at every move. It would be hard to blame Great Britain for leaving some of the fighting to the newest ally, and no one would be less likely to protest than the United States, which entered the war after the worst of the strain was over and can never, in any event, suffer as have those who took up the cudgels earlier.

That there should be a problem in a democratic country of finding the men for a war like this is not surprising. It is no contemptuous comment on the loyalty of the British. No other country would have gone so far on voluntarism, no country have given such proof of its patriotism without coercion. But there comes a limit to voluntarism in a war where every man and woman has work to do; and the shirkers stand out more prominently than their numbers warrant. Where Great Britain failed was in the loopholes she provided to the shirkers. Without preparation she found the men to block the armies of a country trained and fitted to the last movement and gun. It was only in the last pound of her strength that her manhood failed her. She secured the men for the worst days of the war. And even without the entry of later allies she would have found the men for victory when her back was against the wall.

Freedom is a misnomer in a nation's crisis.

The next article of this series is entitled "The Food Problem".

The Food Problem

By W. Lacey Amy
Part VII of 'England in Arms'
From *The Canadian Magazine,* November 1917

To date the problem faced in the feeding of the people of the British Isles is not that of food shortage, but of food distribution. To the foreigner that assertion may seem to deprive the situation of most of its seriousness; to us who live through it and watch its development therein lies more menace than in the expressed hopes of the Kaiser. British ingenuity may be depended upon more confidently to overcome the enemy than to alter internal affairs in order to cope with unusual conditions. Nothing is so powerful against the Englishman as his habits and system.

No one in the British Isles has felt the pinch of hunger. And it is not likely that anyone will. What suffering there has been arises from the temporary shortage of unessentials and from high prices. Sugar and potatoes sum up the total of national deprivations owing to the war, and never did they approach privations because there has always been something to take their places. Before there is actual want the British will have solved the submarine. But after three years of a situation that has continually pointed to food as one of the vital factors in the winning of victory they are only now nearing the solution of a situation with which the enemy has nothing to do— which is, indeed, indigenous to the British race, but more particularly to that section of it residing in England and Scotland.

The problem of distribution is twofold. The limitation of supplies—rather the necessity of conserving for an uncertain future— demands an equality of distribution that ignored individuals and class. The second difficulty is the British character—an independence which resents control and dictation. Of the two the latter was the more immediately dangerous at the beginning of the conservation movement. But common sense is asserting itself, so that equality of distribution now occupies the time of the Food Controller. When he found temperance in eating to be so necessary as to justify Government action, the Englishman yielded to a pressure which he naturally resists. But having yielded, he was forced to set to work on the national system of class favouritism—as, indeed, he has been forced to do in every problem connected with the war.

It was Britain's unquestioned command of the seas that delayed food measures which were reasonable from the very first gun. That inbred and time-honoured confidence in victory laid a heavy hand on reasonable provision and prevision in every act of war. In the matter of food arbitrary measures did not seem to be necessary early in the struggle. Depending entirely, as it did, on the control of the seas, Great Britain was justified in her confidence, a confidence that would never have been shaken had the Germans adhered to the rules of warfare.

One measure only was taken early in the war to protect the food supply of the British Isles, an obvious one immediately demanded by the fact that they had been procuring more than sixty per cent. of their sugar from Germany. A Sugar Commission was appointed. Thereafter, for more than two years, even when the casual onlooker was viewing the situation with alarm and the Asquith Government itself was talking much of plans in the House, nothing further was done. Always in the mind of the people was the thought that the enemy could not drive Great Britain to defensive measures that would reflect upon its special sphere of power; and in the mind of the Government was the hope that political balances need not be disturbed by restrictive action certain to be resented in some quarters. For it must not be imagined that party aims and hopes disappeared with the formation of a Coalition Cabinet.

The second official move of importance was made in October, 1916, when a Wheat Commission undertook to readjust the grain situation. Unfortunately it was weighted down with the Asquith love of laisser-faire, and its duties never materialized into effective action. At a time when the enemy was openly sinking merchant vessels and threatening more, when the demands of military operations and national supply were so deflecting shipping from the ordinary channels of food transportation that reserves of grain in the British Isles were being seriously depleted, no action was taken towards replenishing these supplies from a world's production that was above the normal. America and Australia were offering the grain, but England was not willing to disturb the trend of affairs in order to facilitate the acceptance of the offers.

The press of England was becoming alive to the menace, and the English press has a voice more powerful than that of its brother across the ocean. The people were growing anxious. The difficulty of securing sugar was impressing even the thoughtless with the need for action. Mr. Asquith was forced to promise operations which were loathsome to him, not alone for their antagonism to his policy, but for the danger he well saw would arise therefrom to his personal popularity. He announced the establishment of a new department headed by a Food Controller. It promised well. But the Food Controller was never appointed. Week after week the country waited. Mr. Asquith was at his best in his promises of what that important official would do—in his explanations of the delay. He was at his most natural in his inability to come to the point of action.

It was the accumulation of such dilatory acts as these that brought about his downfall. Just three days before an anxious Cabinet, backed by a roused people, demanded his resignation, Mr. Runciman, one of his Ministers, placed before the country one lone food measure that even then looked like a small mouse for the mountain to bring forth. Restrictions were placed on restaurant fare—or rather attempted restrictions. Luncheon was to be a two-course meal and the ample English restaurant dinner was to be limited to three courses.

With that heritage Lloyd George assumed power. His first discovery in connection with the food situation was that his predecessor had taken no inventory of the nation's supplies, had made no move to simplify the work of the Food Department, which had immediately to be organized. One of the first officials appointed in the new Government was a Food Controller, Lord Devonport, a man whose intimate connection with food supply as the head of a large multiple store company seemed to qualify him for the position. It was a disappointment to the country and to the Premier himself that the seeming qualifications for the Controller's office should in the end prove the insuperable obstacle to his effectiveness. Lord Devonport introduced many measures intended to cope with a situation passing rapidly into a serious stage, but a calm survey of them discovers them to be, after all, paltry, a mere touching of the surface.

Lord Devonport took pleasure in vetoing the Runciman restaurant order four months after it had been put into effect, and almost the same time after its folly had become evident. The limited course meal brought only one result, that diners ate more solid meat, and less of the odds and ends, the entrees and unessentials and make-overs, that give the daintiest touch to restaurant fare without affecting food stocks. Men formerly content with a small helping of meat in the interests of the decorative courses, demanded meat and bread and cheese, the basis of subsistence. The new Food Controller, too, was forced to deal with bread, tea, confectionery, potatoes and other vegetables, and sugar.

His substitute for the Runciman restaurant control was a meatless day and a limitation of the amounts of meat, bread and sugar served at each meal. This was later altered because of its drain on bread in order to take the place of meat on the meatless day. Bread he attempted to regulate by prohibiting its sale until twelve hours after baking, and by limiting its shape, weight and constituents. The adulteration of flour by maize or rice, and the prohibition of the waste that produces white flour, resulted in what is known as war bread. It was an effective measure, despite the continued opposition of the people. Tea—considered in England almost as great a food necessity as bread—was regulated in its cheaper qualities. A curb was put on the use of sugar in confectionery, pastry and icing. In the early part of 1917 potatoes were passing so rapidly into the list of shortages that price limitation was necessary. Three cents a pound for old stock was established for the early months, rising later a half-cent. But no measures could increase the supply, and no attempt was made to prevent the farmers holding their stocks for higher prices. For months it might be said there were no potatoes in England. And with the failure of potatoes the vegetable substitutes advanced until the Food Controller was forced to limit the price of some of them.

Where Lord Devonport failed was in his reluctance to take a firm stand, to enforce the law, and principally to curtail the profits of the trader. He attempted to solve the problem by appeal. A chart of patriotic proportions in the daily diet was flung at the public in a thousand ways. The fences were covered with it, the newspapers gave it daily space, lecturers flooded the country, and, at a time when the shortage of paper was serious, the workingmen's pay envelopes were crammed with a literature he never read. To the credit of the country the consumption of bread and meat materially decreased. But the two insuperable obstacles to success were the inability of ninety per cent. of the people to purchase the advised ration of sugar and the eagerness of some to seize the opportunity for gorging. While there were millions willing to curb their appetites there were flaunting thousands of pro-German sympathies or utter carelessness whose delight it was to evade the appeal and the laws. And at the very time when the people were begged to stint themselves interned and imprisoned Germans were allowed many times the ration; sugar and potatoes were being commandeered for them when the workers of the country had to go without. The inconsistencies of the situation were intolerable, and the effectiveness of the appeal diminished weekly.

In the matter of enforcing the law there was singular laxness. Here and there a dealer was fined, although it was impossible to go on the streets without seeing plainly advertised infractions of the food laws. And the fine was usually but a small part of the profit made from the illicit transaction. Indeed, there was apparent, in store and home and restaurant, a merry revelry of law evasion that undid the patriotism of those who honestly rationed themselves.

Profiteering went on without restriction. Lord Devonport, head of a big grocery concern, persisted in refusing to limit the profits of grocers save in a few glaring and insignificant cases. Swedes, for instance, the substitute for potatoes, were limited in price to three cents a pound, a price so many times what the farmer and greengrocer had been receiving that neither could complain. The setting of prices for potatoes and beans was much advertised but unimportant, for both disappeared from the market almost immediately. Although the cost of bread to miller and baker was materially decreased by the new laws, the price advanced instantly to the consumer two to four cents a four-pound loaf. While a few bakers outside London were content with the profits from seventeen-cent bread, the London baker charged twenty-four. The attempt to democratize tea was a failure. Forty per cent. of the importations were to be sold to the public at fifty-two and fifty-six cents, but no one was ever able to purchase a pound of the cheaper price, to my knowledge, and if the better quality of Government tea was inquired for it was either out of stock or sneered at by the grocer. Neither price was ever displayed in the windows during Lord Devonport's term. The same happened with cheese. A large part of it was taken over by the Government to be sold over the counter for thirty-two cents, but it never appeared on the shelves of more than a very few stores.

With meat no attempt was made to interfere until the last days of Lord Devonport's office, and then only the speculator was eliminated, the retailer being permitted to ask what he pleased. Of the retailers the butcher was the most heartless profiteer, the consumer being asked sixty to one hundred and fifty per cent. profit over the wholesale prices. Even the supplies controlled by the Government, such as New Zealand mutton, were turned loose upon arrival in England for the wholesaler and retailer to make what profit he wished. Laid down in London by the Government at thirteen cents, it reached the public at thirty-six to sixty cents. The butcher could not buy it without a large purchase of English mutton at extravagant prices. And in the meantime, in order to maintain the level of prices, tons of meat were left to rot on the docks.

There is no better example of the injudicious and unfair distribution of supplies than sugar, the commodity that has induced several crises already. To the people the only result of the Sugar Commission was an immediate rise in price. Against this there has been constant complaint, for it is known that the rise represented taxation and Government profit. It was not until the latter part of 1916 that a shortage began seriously to be felt; but from the first pinch the shortage increased until stocks seemed to have disappeared from the market, so far as the poorer classes were concerned. By December women were walking the streets from shop to shop begging half-pounds. Queues had not then commenced, because sugar was the only shortage and the grocer sold only to whom he liked.

It is this independence of the merchant that has driven home to the country the disaster of typical official control, so called. Each week the Sugar Commission released to the wholesalers their shares of the available supplies, and washed their hands of any further connection with the commodity. Theoretically the wholesaler was supposed to pass on to the grocer his share, but that he had favourites is proved by the fact that some of the large West End stores seemed never to be without sugar, while the small grocer of the East End was denied a pound. It must be remembered that every pound of sugar shipped to England was Government-controlled. No control whatever was exercised over the retailer save in the matter of price, and the shortage of the available supplies enabled him to make sugar the basis of his trade. He sold to whom he pleased in the quantities he pleased. His independence became impudence. A customer was always a beggar, for he was entirely at the mercy of his grocer. Sugar was denied those who could not afford to make their purchases extravagant. Some system seemed to arrive with the demand for a purchase of fifty cents' worth of other goods with each half-pound or pound of sugar, and this was accepted by the authorities as a wise provision against wasteful purchases of the limited commodity. It was the strength of class in England that for many months prevented the authorities from realizing that such a stipulation reserved sugar for the rich who could afford to buy supplies they did not need in order to obtain the sugar they did. It was only when the merchants began to extend the same demand to the purchase of other foodstuffs that the Government forbade any conditions with the sale of sugar. But the grocer was still left to sell to whom he pleased. No improvement whatever resulted, since the grocer simply refused to sell until another large order was given.

The cry of the poor—the long, hopeless queues, the untrained cooks helpless to provide for their large families without that which had made up such a large part of their food—was pitiful. And all the time the West End shops were selling it in fifty-pound lots or less. The Government's loose effort to enable fruit-growers to preserve their fruit was equally unfair. The growers sent in their requirements, and the sugar was released to the grocer mentioned in the requisition, but without any control over the amount he passed on to the grower. Of four friends, no two received the same proportion of that which they had asked for, the amount varying from fifty to ninety per cent. No one knows what the grocer should have given out. The latest measure in the handling of sugar, to come into force in October, is a form of card supply, but still there is no safeguard that the grocer will sell to his customers their individual shares of the available supplies.

The clamorous protest arising was more than threatening. Lord Devonport accepted the inevitable and resigned. Lord Rhondda assumed the thankless job. It is typical of English public life that only a titled man is considered competent to undertake public work. The war has introduced a Geddes or two; others will have to follow. Particularly unfortunate in the matter of controlling resources is this habit, since these wealthy titled men are so closely concerned in a financial way with the industries and commerce of the country that unprejudiced outlook is nigh to impossible. Lord Rhondda had made good in his first Government office and in private life, and initiative was not lacking. His misfortune was that he was appointed at a time when public impatience would not brook delay. Without time to study the situation and devise methods he was driven to instant action. The result was a hundred more or less vague promises that seemed to fit in with the demands of the people, and one act only of the immediate future. Profiteering was the bête noire of the people, and on profiteering he came out strong—in word. Thus far there is only the promise that profiteering will be punished by imprisonment. Speculation is to be stopped, how is not apparent. Lord Devonport had already issued orders to that effect in the case of meat without affecting much the price to the consumer. The only definite act which would tend to soothe the people was an obvious expedient. It dealt with the commodity most familiar to the table—bread. Bread was ordered to be sold—some time in the future—at eighteen cents a quartern loaf.

Realizing that the British Isles might be called upon to depend upon their own resources, he turned to the farmer. Land was tilled that had never been broken for centuries, and the farmer became a real producer. If he didn't, there was a law to take his land from him temporarily. Ploughing was done by tractor, night and day and Sundays. The added crop acreage was expected to amount to millions, but lack of tractors and help and quick co-operation reduced the amount to less than half a million acres. Next year the millions are promised. Allotments sprang up everywhere—vacant lots, golf links, railway tracks, parks. London alone is producing eight hundred extra acres of vegetables. The additional growth has reduced the price of potatoes for the moment to less than it was before the war; and the absence of market organization is leaving tons to rot, England was driven to act before she could complete the organization necessary to reap the greatest reward.

The solution does not yet appear. If the submarine continues even its present success, and the measures of the future do not improve substantially on those of the past, the British Isles will feel want. Private profits, private shipping, block all the Government can do. The controlling influences of supply and demand are non-existent in time of war. With Government interference they lost almost all their power, in all justice. To continue that power is to exploit the Government of the people at the cost of the people. To-day the old tenet of the economist means nothing more, in the case of importations, than to ask the people, at their own expense, to make trade possible by import regulations and transportation protection, and then to expect them to pay the trader according to the volume and expense of that protection. And locally-grown products are directly dependent for price, especially in England, on the available stocks from without.

The stopping of profiteering is a pleasant ambition to talk about but an over-lofty one to anticipate. Profiteering does not end with the grocer and butcher, the wholesaler and shipper. It has entered into every phase of home life. Only the man in khaki, who assumes all the risk of war, is precluded from it. The workingman, the clerk, the farmer, the thousands of Government officials who have risen with the war—even the Government itself—are profiting from the war. But the burden is uneven. The workingman of England can present a good defence in terms of comparative wage scale, but in terms of total receipt—which is the basis of his living—he might be called a profiteer. His five pence an hour of pre-war days may have increased only sixty per cent., while living has advanced one hundred; but his week's envelope contains probably three times—often six and ten times—what it did before the war. The decreased facilities for drink and idleness keep him longer at work, and the additions of bonus and overtime are not infrequently greater than his regular wage.

The next article of this series will discuss the elaborate plans being made in England for the conservation of materials.

Conservation of Materials

By W. Lacey Amy
Part VIII of the series 'England in Arms'
From *The Canadian Magazine,* December 1917.

IT required the war to convince the most patriotic of us that Great Britain was year by year becoming less self-contained, that by processes subtle or open her rivals in the world's commerce, especially Germany, were gradually ousting her not alone from the foreign markets but from her own. And in the revelation that came with war one more economic theory received a staggering blow that manufacture of specific commodities should be left to the countries in a position to produce them most economically. The theory was unassailable were peace a permanent blessing. But war has a habit of uprooting theory with relentless hand. There still remain in England those who resist the apparent corollary, that unprofitable national production must be protected, but the teachings of war are rendering their ideals at least momentarily unobtrusive. The grim straits through which Great Britain has passed since August, 1914, have impressed her with the national helplessness that accompanies the relinquishment to foreign countries of national necessities. And as manufacturers are not the class who willingly produce at a loss in competition with their foreign rivals, there exists only the solution of Government protection in some form.

Great Britain never realized how the very essentials of life were drifting into the hands of the Germans, until the sudden closing of the German market forced her to review her own industry. The facts forced home to her might well have discouraged another less resourceful country. Not alone were the needs of everyday life unfulfillable, but some of the very weapons of war had so subtly trickled from British control that only British brain was able to cope with the situation without more than a temporary setback. Perhaps had the war been delayed ten years British brain might not have been so ready to re-grapple with a production she had lost only for a few years.

It is the popular impression that German dyes represent the climax of British dependence, but the dyes themselves are the least material of the deficiencies of British production. Not yet has the

140

dominance of Germany in this commercial commodity been overcome, but adaptable substitutes are readily available, and dyes are in their nature immaterial to national victory or even national life. Where the German monopoly of dyestuffs looms most awkwardly is in the fact that Great Britain did not grasp their real significance as an indirect factor in international relations; for Germany's monopoly was the result of her preparations for war, not of her superior inventive powers, the basis for dyes being the by-product of the manufacture of munitions. German dyes were subsidized in order to utilize the coal-tar resulting from certain munition-making processes, and every dye-works was instantly convertible in time of war to war services. Dyes, therefore, have been the least of Great Britain's troubles in the war.

In a thousand household needs Britain's dependence became revealed almost with the declaration of war, and some of these were of sufficient importance to demand official attention at the same time as the more intimate ones of munition production. Since their manufacture has been permitted to creep into German hands more as an economic measure than through any inability to fulfil the local needs, they presented no striking problem. But in a score of the prime requirements of war the effect was different. Certain processes of steel manufacture suitable for munitions were not practised in England. Electric supplies for Great Britain came almost entirely from our enemies. In the outskirts of London to-day lies idle an incomplete electric railway, because construction was in the hands of German engineers using German fittings and principles. The little magnetoes that are essential to the aeroplane and the automobile were so completely of German manufacture that even to-day they are produced in England by only two or three firms and their efficiency and cost is still not such as to supplant the German article should open competition recommence immediately. Germany was selling Great Britain all her finer grades of glass, such as those used for lenses and laboratory purposes. Great Britain had even permitted Germany to enter her distant possessions for the practical monopolization of the minerals used in the working of steel processes. For her finer machinery required in the production of munitions Great Britain is to-day at the mercy of America, since the English working engineer has not yet arrived at that nicety of adjustment, that perfection of specification which is absolutely necessary for serviceable and reliable instruments of war. I admit it with reluctance but with certainty of my ground. Indeed, English manufacturers are candid in their statements that they must still look to America for the mechanical delicacy and nicety which have made British munition production one of the marvels of the war. This they may well leave where it is for the present, so long as Britain's energies are completely utilized for more immediate requirements. Its unsatisfactory feature is that this very mechanical perfection will be as essential to much of the coming industrial struggle of peace as it is now to the war output.

Toys, dolls, metal and leather novelties, gas mantles, brushes, certain popular earthenware, office requisites, musical instruments— these are a few of her daily wants for which Great Britain had been wont to send her travellers to the great German markets, such as were represented at the Leipsic Fair.

There were other disadvantages under which Britain laboured on account of her insular position. For her timber she was dependent largely on Norway, Sweden and Russia, and to a less degree on America. The skins for her leather came for the great part from abroad. Her paper was the product of foreign pulp. Her metals arrived by boat. In the bulkier raw materials England may be said to have been self-supporting only in coal.

Her problems would have been simple, even in the face of these deficiencies, had it not been for the submarine warfare adopted by the enemy. British control of the seas and of the shipping covering them would have assured her of sufficient supplies for her every want. The demands for war transportation would have embarrassed her shipping capacity to such a small extent that the simplest expedients of conservation would have sufficed. But with the sinkings and delays of unrestricted warfare conservation became a question equally vital with the protection of the merchant shipping and the upkeep of the army. How she went about it is peculiar to a nation, proud, bound by tradition, reluctant to admit even inconvenience—and certain to overcome in the final emergency.

With the requisitioning of tonnage for war purposes—the transportation of soldiers, wounded, and supplies; patrolling the coasts, mine-sweeping, auxiliary cruiser duties—the necessity for some control of importations became evident. Certain luxuries were gradually eliminated from the freight lists, the bulkier unessentials first. A part of the tonnage was requisitioned for stated importations at Government rates. But the inadequacy of these measures became apparent long before the sinkings were numerous enough to be an immediate menace, and the injustice of singling out a few ships and depriving them of the high rates obtainable by free ships clamoured for redress. In addition, it gradually impressed itself on the nation that any satisfactory solution of the submarine menace entailed a more perfect organization for the elimination of delay in loading and unloading, as well as the speeding up of construction. For these purposes experienced officials were appointed. Construction was not only standardized, but workmen were utilized where they were of greatest service, irrespective of firms and employers. The difficulty of delays in loading was met to some extent by mobile dockers' battalions, and by a more strict supervision of transportation and labour.

But shipping cannot be said to have been brought within the scope of a thorough control until the middle of 1917, when the Government took over ninety-seven per cent. of the entire British registry at Government rates. By this means it was not only assured of reasonable freight charges, but the entire capacity of the boats was directed with a sole eye to the real requirements of the situation. The move took the place of the scores of former regulations. It became no longer a case of publishing prohibited importations but of satisfying the Government that purchases abroad were in the interests of the country at large. Every British liner was taken over, and the profits derived from private freight went to the nation. The result was a pooling of interests by the large transportation companies. Long voyages gave place to short substitutes, and the facilities of the nearest ports were always available to save time. Shipowners arranged to purchase their ships' stores and provisions abroad in order to save home stocks—an obvious act of wisdom that was so little recognized even during the early months of 1917 that Spanish and Dutch and Norwegian vessels were continuing their custom of drawing their supplies from English ports. At the very moment when not a pound of potatoes was finding its way to the majority of tables in Great Britain these foreign ships were taking away with them thousands of tons.

Land transportation, while not in the same emergent class as shipping, entered the scheme of conservation on account of the shortage of men, and because trucks and engines had been requisitioned for the use of the army in France. This was effected by reducing passenger service to the minimum, and by organizing delivery so that the shortest route and distance was compulsory. For instance, coal was brought to London only from the nearest mines and by the shortest line, the railways being brought under Government control to a disinterested co-operation. One striking failure to complete the simplification of transportation was in the neglect of the canals that cut England in every direction. Whether this was owing to their railway ownership or to Governmental thoughtlessness is not clear, but such bulky freight as coal might have been poured into London by this means of transportation without disturbing the material so much in demand for quicker delivery.

The immediate need for metals and explosive ingredients for war purposes, as well as for other commodities hitherto imported, drove England to measures never before contemplated. The Explosives Department of the Ministry of Munitions was organized to assume the duty of acquiring the necessary raw material of explosives. Glycerine was early placed on the controlled lists, and in February, 1917, was further restricted to preparations of the British Pharmacopoeia and to uses approved by the Ministry. It was practically eliminated from dispensing. In March, the shortage being serious, a special branch of the Explosives Department was formed to take over control of all fats, oils, oil-seeds, and their products, including oilcake, soap, and margarine. For the same purpose the waste of camp canteens and messes has been carefully collected for more than a year. Since one of the by-products in the manufacture of illuminating gas is a necessity for explosives, the people were urged to use gas where possible for heat, light and power. The huge demand for petrol led to the Government resuming the long-interrupted efforts to find oil in Great Britain, and in order to prevent exploitation the Crown assumed the exclusive right to bore. Should petroleum be discovered in quantity— and there have been signs that point to success—the submarine menace will be nearer to solution than it has ever been. The same prospecting is being undertaken for metals, although it is certain that only small supplies of inferior quality will be found, lead and zinc comprising the bulk of British possibilities. Copper was requisitioned in December, 1916, and its use for manufacturing purposes forbidden.

The control of petrol has been one of the big failures of attempted conservation. For the first twenty months of the war this control rested in the hands of various inter-departmental committees whose main anxiety—as is the case in a hundred instances of divided control in England—was their authority and dignity. They competed against each other in the market and in shipping facilities and bought in the application of their authority even in war spheres. The Petrol Committee which succeeded them had not a petrol expert in its composition, and at its best was impeded by a jealous Board of Trade. In disgust it resigned, after a period of inadequate control and incompetent efforts. Its successor has proved more efficient. A different scheme has evolved. The principal petroleum companies have arranged a pool for distribution and importation, under the control of a Pool Board Petroleum Supplies. Restrictions were early put on petrol licences, and these have been extended at various times with the declared aim of cutting out private consumption. Business firms are allowed a certain amount for delivery purposes. Taxi-cabs, of which there were 8,287 in London alone before the war, were reduced to an allowance of thirty gallons a month, the most conspicuous result of which was to encourage the drivers to break the laws governing their service to the public. And motor-buses, which provide the popular means of transportation in London, were seriously curtailed. But the working of the restrictions was glaringly lax and unfair. Petrol was wasted in the army sometimes used even for washing the trucks. Taxis, which usually carry but one passenger, were granted petrol which if supplied to the interrupted bus service would have carried many times the number of passengers. Until recently there were no restrictions whatever on the motor luxuries of officers, every one of whom of any rank has his own car and chauffeur for running about England. Day and night and Sundays this indulgence was unlimited until the middle of 1917, and since then its control has been evident only in the replies of Government officers before the House of Commons. While private licences were supposed to be cut off in May, 1917, there is not a minute of the day when any important street in London does not prove that civilians still ride at their pleasure; and on Sundays the roads from London are still busy. In spite of the repeated official denials that petrol is granted for private use there is the frankest display of such waste. Even the social notes in the newspapers speak of wedding trips and visits to seaside resorts by motor, and the procuring of supplies demands but slight ingenuity. The greatest obstacle to such a perversion of a much-needed commodity is a price of $1.17 a gallon established in August, only twelve cents of which is Government tax. It is a detail of the recognized principle of regulation in England to reserve the privileges for the rich.

The shortage of petrol has led to the use of substitutes, but the further prohibition of liquid substitutes has confined the inventiveness of motor enthusiasts to the utilization of gas.

Conservation of coal has been taken up officially, not because of a national shortage, but to save labour and transportation. In 1915 the price was fixed to prevent exploitation. In the spring of 1917 there was in London a severe shortage that bore heavily on the poor, who purchase in small quantities; and in the summer of that year steps were taken to prevent a repetition. A Coal Controller was appointed to arrange delivery from the nearest mines and to equalize distribution. The Board of Trade issued advice to the people to purchase their winter supplies early, but when the orders poured in it was found there was not the coal to fill them. It was another instance of neglected preliminary organization before urging the public to action. The several instances of this which have occurred have done much to discourage public co-operation in attempted conservation. The next step was to ration the coal according to the number of grates. A house with not more than four grates was allowed two hundredweight a week, and the allotment was detailed up to two tons and a half for a house of more than fifteen rooms. Every consumer using more than two hundredweight a week had to register. The Controller's plan was to work up to a five weeks' stock in the coal yards, reducing the allowance as this quantity was reduced. The difficulties of such a system of rationing are obvious, since the extent of occupation of a house, rather than its number of grates, determines its consumption. There is, too, no assurance that the rationed quantity will be available.

One of the early materials to be controlled was paper. Newspapers were cut down to definite quantities, based on their consumption during the year before the war, and this amount was further reduced in 1916. Importation was in the hands of the Government. The result was a dwindling of size and a consequent increase in price owing to the curtailment of advertising space. *The Times* rose by halfpenny stages to twopence, and many of the halfpenny papers advanced to a penny. In March, 1917, posters over a certain size were forbidden, and tradesmen might not send out catalogues or price lists except on request. The newspaper contents bill, a feature of street announcement in England, was prohibited. By the last measure alone it is estimated that 500 tons a week are saved. In July, 1917, the War Office arranged that, since the casualty lists could no longer be published in the smaller papers, they should be issued weekly to the bookstores for sale. A few days later tradesmen were limited in their circulars and catalogues to a third the weight of paper used in the same period of the year before. And the whiteness of paper has been sacrificed in order to save bleaching powder.

In the matter of wearing apparel control was delayed as long as possible. Leather had first to be taken in hand. The huge call for army boots was eating into the available supplies with disturbing rapidity, and in March, 1917, the Government took over all sole and upper leathers suitable for army use, following a less complete requisition of the previous December. Civilian footwear immediately advanced. In June the Government made arrangements for the sale of old army boots at fixed centres, with the stipulation that they should not be patched but taken to pieces for repairing other shoes. The object was to prevent the scrapping of serviceable army boots. But shoe repairs continued to rise so seriously—soling advanced more than three hundred per cent. from the period before the war—that in September the Government was forced once more to intervene and release for civilian use at fixed prices quantities of leather suitable for repairs.

An Advisory Committee on Wool Purchase was set up, representing the various Government departments concerned and civilian interests. It fixed prices and prescribed uses. Wool was not largely imported, but it was deemed advisable to continue exports as well as to supply home needs. Standard cloth is now produced for officers' uniforms, and civilian wear will probably be similarly controlled. The manufacture of cotton has had to be curtailed, although it is one of England's leading manufactures. Blankets are in Government control for army use and only such quantities released for civilian use as are considered necessary.

All stocks of sawn timber in the United Kingdom were taken over by the Government in February, 1917, and in July the Local Government Board urged local authorities to forgo the use of wood-paving for the period of the war. In January anastigmatic lenses of defined focal lengths were requisitioned. In February the supplies of jute in the country were commandeered. In June citizens were requested by the Board of Trade not to waste glass receptacles of any kind. Metal spur, chains, buttons and badges of rank on officers' uniforms were abolished, leather spur straps and buttons, and worsted badges of rank taking their place. Stone quarries were taken over in July.

General prevention of waste and of misdirection of effort was applied in a score of ways. Building and private motor-making were stopped. A new Bill was introduced for the prevention of corruption in Government contracts. A department was set up for the utilization of idle machinery. In 1916 an Order-in-Council empowered the Admiralty and Army Council to regulate or prohibit transactions in any article required in connection with the war. No horse suitable for cultivation of land might be sold by the land occupier without licence. To save fuel illuminated advertisements and lights outside shops and theatres were prohibited in May. 1917. In extension of this principle two of the large London stores closed on Saturdays.

Of course, with all this evident shortage there was profiteering. The case of matches affords a good example. These sold before the war as low as three cents a dozen boxes. Today they are as high as thirty-two cents, although the manufacturers insist that not more than sixteen cents should be asked the consumer. In addition to their high price there are times when they cannot be obtained at all, and the stores release to each customer only a small box or two. The Government, knowing there were sufficient stocks somewhere, has taken steps to control distribution. A pool of manufacturers has been formed, and orders will be taken only through a Match Control Office in London, which will be under the Tobacco Control Board.

In these measures of conservation it was necessary at times to ignore the claims even of allied countries. France, being close at hand and Great Britain's source for much that might be called luxuries, has suffered most keenly. Fruit, wine, and silk were the largest of these importations. At various times all these products of our friends across the Channel have been either restricted or prohibited. Protest has been made, and at times mild reprisals applied, but common sense has prevailed. In some cases the protesting country yielded, in others the restrictions were modified. A general agreement between the two countries was announced in September. By it England takes from France goods of French origin, except such as wood, motor-cars, machinery, gold, spirits, and ornamental goods; and France has thrown her doors open to everything but cotton and woollen piece goods, soap, and oils. The fact that England has the European Allies almost completely at her mercy on account of her control of shipping is proof of the wisdom and justice of her treatment of them.

The straits into which the war has thrown Great Britain in the matter of material supplies are not without their blessing. The people of the small island which has dominated the world for so many centuries are learning how luxurious and enervating was their style of life among certain classes, how much they can eliminate without serious inconvenience—even with advantage—and how near they were to losing valuable markets. The necessities of war have developed an inventiveness that was tending to doze and have taught the wisdom of greater dependence on their own productions than upon those of other countries who appraise more truly the value of industrial eminence in the world's markets. England after the war will swing swiftly into the England she can be, a resourceful country that need give precedence to no rival in commercial as well as in intellectual attainments.

The next article of this series is entitled "The Enemy in England".

The Enemy in England

By W. Lacey Amy
Part IX of the series 'England in Arms'.
From *The Canadian Magazine,* January 1918.

IT is not inconsistent, though it is unfortunate, that those charac-
teristics which, in time of peace, are counted to a nation's credit, in
time of war oft-times stand to its disservice and mischief. Bound into
the very foundation on which the British Empire was built, close,
indeed, to its keystone, is tolerence; just as, sooner or later, the first
crumbling breach in the walls of German resistance will show where
intolerance has been so prominently fixed. But as even a virtue,
uncontrolled, may approach a vice, so Britain's (especially England's)
acceptance of the widest application of tolerance, in a time when little
counts but the life of the nation and the sternest support of those great
principles which focus only in the defeat of an inhuman foe, has
become to it in certain stages of the war a menace it should not have
risked. And yet it is so much easier to moralize than to follow the
straight path of virtue as demanded by the altered conditions of war
that history is not apt to sum up England's part in the war as a careless
disregard for the sensible precautions that consider only victory.

Behind England's calm tolerance of the enemy in its midst stand
the principles of government that have held together an Empire more
diverse than ever before was bound together even by the thinnest
threads. The ancient Romans, whose dominion was more ambitious
but infinitely less effective and extensive, never attempted the feat of
welding such confusion of tongue, such diversity of character, such
uncongenial spirits as Great Britain has governed without serious
strife for generations Necessarily it had perforce to be a government
of indulgence, of concessions, of licence. To weave into one fabric
the Scotsman and the Indian and the Chinese, and the hundred distinct
units of a hundred corners of the world, imprinted that on the English
character which has made him a cosmopolite. It has opened his mind
to a thousand vagaries of individual belief. It has opened his hand to
the puny communities of distant sections which would have been
beneath the notice of any other nation. It has opened its doors to the
world's refugees—which means not alone the world's downtrodden
but its criminals, its outcasts, its great unwanted. And with the

150

unlimited opening has grown up an intolerance of intolerance, a firm reputation of the closed corporation, in national as in commercial life. Only in his private life does the Englishman cling to the barriers.

England became a haven, built in those principles. The Anarchists of France and Spain and Italy found a home there; the Nihilists of Russia fled there before the sword of unrelenting Czarism; the political outcasts of a score of countries swarmed to the little island that refused to give them up to the avenging hand of their own countries. And, more dangerous than all, the spies of the nations that train spies as a feature of the national system, found there their mart of exchange, their delving ground, their most profitable source of the information which might some day be used against the country that gave them shelter. It has always been presented as the best justification of this attitude that the Anarchist and the political exiles who harbour there have thrown aside their dangerous tenets in their relationship to England. But it is a defence which has been repudiated more often than has been made public and from which countries friendly to Great Britain have suffered almost without protest. When Winston Churchill turned machine guns on the foreign criminals of a street in East-End London he was but laying the foundation for an enlightenment which has been spreading over England since the greatest war in history revealed new national principles. But tolerance died hard. Indeed, it is not dead, though the Empire pays for it in human blood.

One must let these truths penetrate in any examination of the treatment that has been meted to the enemy alien in England. No nation, and especially not England, can throw aside the principles of generations that have built up such an Empire. Add thereto the sporting instincts of the Englishman, the desire to give even the most powerful and menacing enemy the privileges of open combat, and there opens up something of the reasons behind the leniency which met the German and the Austrian and the Turk who had found their homes in the British Isles. Consider therewith, too, the freedom of action which these foreigners enjoyed for so long that they had been able to make themselves powers in the land, backed by the official support of their own governments, aided by the co-operation of a million fellow-countrymen in other parts of the world. These men had wormed their way into the very national framework, of finance and industry and commerce, even into politics. They had stormed society with gold and kingly honours. They had married their sons and daughters to English daughters and sons, often, it is certain, merely in pursuit of the common aim of influence. They had won or purchased staunchest friends, in civil as in political life. They held many of the imposing properties which commanded respect and subservience as ancient rights. In the House of Commons were ardent defenders whose honesty has never been impugned, as well as a few others whose motives might well be questioned.

So that when the war broke out they had behind them the English wall of tradition, the firm support of influential friends, the trust of the powers who alone could curtail their liberties, and the pride of the Englishman who disdains to excite himself over any peril. They were many times entrenched.

To the man on the street it would seem to be the part of wisdom instantly to protect the nation against the machinations of the enemy resident. But the man on the street finds the way to action long. Canada, as well as England, has been indulgent to the German in its midst. The politician is bound by different views, by different motives and necessities. It happened that in the British House at the outbreak of war the Home Office was under one whose sympathies were loyal enough but more actively tolerant. Indeed, the head of the office has at all times concerned himself with the enemy alien and his rights and protection more than is agreeable to the public and to his fellow Ministers. It may be more the fault of the estimated duties of the office than of the man himself. With the declaration of war nothing was done to control the spy. Evidences of his handiwork were not only suspected but revealed in a score of cases. Prominent Germans, known to be in the favour of the Kaiser, were afforded their customary liberties. Enemy firms whose interests were wholly German were permitted to conduct their businesses along the usual lines. England, with its eyes firmly fixed on the star of its lofty principle in entering the war, was far above the crude pettiness of individual coercion and limitation. Glowing speeches, that might have sounded well in history had Great Britain won the war during the first four months, were delivered by the page to convince the public that we were waging war on Kaiserism, not on the individual German. It sounded well, but the public was going by sight not by sound. And in the meantime the individual German in many cases was doing his utmost for Kaiserism.

The state of public opinion early in the war drove the resident Germans and Austrians by the hundred to take out naturalization papers; and, according to the law, there was nothing to prevent. The Schmitzs became plain Joneses, and the German signs on the fronts of scores of shops gave place to good old British names without changing proprietors. Protest by the press was met by lifted hands of helplessness. The announced determination of the German rulers to exact retribution from those Germans who did not remain true to their homeland, the declaration that a German could secure naturalization in a foreign country without affecting his German nationality, had no effect on the stand of the authorities.

Only when the Zeppelins in early 1915, dropped death on innocent Britons and friendly foreigners did the public take the course of events into its own hands. Each raid was followed by rioting in the East-End of London that threatened much more than the destruction of a few German shops or injury to a few Germans. To hold the mob in check the Government was forced to take steps to intern 20,000 Germans and Austrians throughout England. In haste the internments were decided upon, but it was noticeable that only the uninfluential Germans were touched, with here and there one of note to make the total bulk large. The relegation to private life of the Prince of Battenberg from his position of authority in the navy early in the war was but one of these act's of pandering to public clamour without realizing the justice of the protest. At the time the internments commenced there was established an Advisory Committee whose duties have apparently been to find ground for excusing prominent Germans from internment, not to intern. In all the list of angry queries which have been thrown at the Government by enthusiastic Britons in the House, there are remarkably few replies pointing to internment upon the advice of this committee, while every German at large has been protected by its reported findings. All over England well-known Germans went about their daily work, not quietly and inoffensively, but boastfully. Many instances have been quoted of a sneering ridicule of their enemies. "They can't intern me" has been hurled by impudent Germans in the face of angry fathers whose sons have died through the release of information that can have been obtained only through spies.

In the time of Asquith the German in England fared exceedingly well. Only after persistent pursuit by the press was he interned, and from his comfortable quarters in Donnington Hall or in the other elaborate quarters where he was semi-controlled, he looked out upon an England disturbed and suffering from a war that inconvenienced him little. He was clothed and fed and waited upon as few Englishmen. His wife was paid an allowance of from five to ten shillings a week more than that allowed the wife of the British soldier fighting in France. His business was run for him, either by an English deputy who paid him the profits, or he was permitted occasional freedom to oversee it. In the two years and more of the Asquith war Premiership scarcely a German business was closed down, although hundreds of them were theoretically under control. Asquith's lax methods made action repugnant, in spite of the constant protest of an influential press. To be sure Enemy Trading Acts were introduced, intended to prevent enemy profit, but there was nothing to prevent a Briton carrying on the business and piling up the profits to be paid the German proprietor after the war is over. Many of these German firms even secured large contracts from the Government at the expense of the British firms.

The entry of Lloyd George into the field promised more than it effected. He found himself faced by a people more intent on the noise of protest than an effective action to satisfy that protest. They saw and resented the freedom of the enemy in the country and to some extent backed the steps necessary to curtail it; but the ways of the country intervened, and had it not been for papers like the Northcliffe press there would have been little more done than to intern a few powerless merchants who had thus far escaped. Then, too, the Court of Appeal came to the protection of the German. Taking advantage of the laws of the land—laws he would have laughed at in his own country— many a German secured his liberty. The Court of Appeal declared that a German at large in England is not an enemy alien, and debts were collected on the strength of it. Lloyd George did, without delay, place in internment several of the best known Germans whose immunity hitherto had been a matter of marvel and whose brazenness threatened a popular uprising. But always there was evident a desire more to appease the public than to effect a public benefit. From the beginning the coercion of German subjects and naturalized Germans has been with a view to exercising official control as little as possible.

The Home Office, driven by a group of influential Britons whose sympathies from the first have been with Germany, has undertaken the care of the German resident, and Lloyd George's administration has altered this attitude little. Official appeals were sent all over the country for firms to engage interned aliens. There was, no doubt, the excuse that it would save the expense of internment, but there was far more the danger that these men, who had been considered dangerous enough to look away from the public, would be able to resume most of their former activities and opportunities for evil; and there was the subtle folly of securing good jobs for a foe whose relentless style of warfare placed them beyond more than mere human consideration. The move was discounted from the first by the indignant refusal of employers to throw open their shops to the enemy.

A committee had been formed early in the war for the benefit of the alien enemy, its funds provided by some of the best known naturalized Germans, German admirers and pacifists. In the list were included such significant names as Haldane, Beit, a prominent Government Official, and the Cadbury Brothers. The influence of the latter was great. As the proprietors of two London daily papers, they had been insistently declaring from the first rumours of war that it was impossible, that Britain misunderstood Germany; and ever since, as Quakers, they have been edging towards peace at every stage where such a word dare be mentioned. Public disgust expressed itself most effectively when a county Prisoners of War Committee returned Mr. B. Cadbury (these are the Cadburys of cocoa fame) the five pounds he had contributed, on the ground that they could not accept it in the face of a personal contribution of £750 and a firm contribution of £1,500 to the funds for interned and uninterned aliens. This pro-enemy committee was constantly at work endeavouring to ease the lot of the enemy alien, soliciting work for him, purchasing luxuries denied our prisoners in Germany, and generally presenting his case to the authorities and the public.

The matter of German businesses walked the same uncertain course under the new Premier. Here and there a German business that had been much in the public eye was closed, but until the press took up a case nothing was done to it. The English manager of Bradstreet's, German born, continued to sign the firm's letters, although theoretically supplanted, until the folly of it was exposed in the press. Of the German banks which had been closing for almost three years one was finally wound up. But in this act, too, was evidenced the unduly favourable treatment accorded the enemy. In strict British fairness, debts owing the German firms were set against their own debts; yet it developed that, while the British debtor was forced to pay 20s. on the pound, the British creditor received only 13s. 4d. The German debts, incurred when the mark stood at 20.40 per £, were paid at an existing rate of 30.45, although at the moment there might be sufficient assets to pay at the full rate; and no one seemed to be able to state how the rate was established.

Failing to find places for the interned Germans in British firms, many were allowed freedom to reopen or manage their former businesses. Others were freed for no apparent reason but that they might resume their former methods of life, living on their incomes. Here and there Germans who had been interned reappeared in their old haunts without public explanation. For some of these someone had gone bail, others were allowed out for a sort of holiday, and still others were released on the word of influential friends or for unknown reasons. The lot of those left in internment continued to be comfortable. At the time when the country was rationing itself, the Germans in Donnington Hall and Alexandra Palace were allowed much larger food supplies, and only when protest was made in the House was a change introduced. To-day, when thousands of homes are unable to secure coal through transportation difficulties Alexandra Palace is amply stocked. An example of superlative kindness to the German is that in Donnington Hall there are 115 servants to wait on 389 German officers.

And still there were at the middle of 1917 about 22,000 Germans and Austrians at large, less than half of them women; and at the last returns given in the House several thousands were living in areas that are called prohibited, where the most valuable information is obtainable. One prominent German purchased recently through his son an estate within a mile of a hill commanding a wide view over the sea, and in the House it was stated that he had been already fined for trading with the enemy and his son for showing a bright light at night. An uninterned German was arrested with important secret military documents and an officer's kit bag in his possession, with German calling-up papers in his pocket. A celebrated Austrian painter has only now been taken into custody (his case was fought out before the advisor committee), although he became naturalized only after war was declared and at the time a letter of his in friends in Austria told of his reluctance to seem thus to repudiate the land of his birth, as well of his enmity to "the predatory Serbian nation". A German was shot by an officer for intrigues with the latter's wife, after the police had known for months of his origin and his association with a woman executed as a spy. Two foundations of German monks were until recently allowed complete freedom in England. On the very day the papers announced a fine of £100 against a British engineer for attempting to purchase without a permit a pistol for experimenting, the English Consul-General for Montenegro arrived at a summer resort in England with an Austrian valet who had been exempted from internment by the Home Office. Several German women have been found doing service in the homes of British officers. The British wife of an interned German was recently lightly fined for attempting to purchase an aeroplane seating four and capable of flying to Germany. As there are many German escaped officers still at large the affair assumed a serious aspect.

Even the Government itself seemed disposed to do its best in its own departments for the Germans. In the central telegraph office were, at one time since the middle of 1917, eight men, in addition to Belgians, not British-born. A young man who claimed exemption from military service on the ground that his parents were German was found employed in a Government telegraph office, through which the most important secrets passed, although substitutes offered themselves. The assistant constructor at an important dockyard was the son of a German father and had visited Germany shortly before the war. A naturalized German was permitted to live close to a large aerodrome. The Minister of Blockades appealed for the exemption of a young German on its staff—and the tribunal granted it. A man of German descent was appointed British Commercial Attaché at The Hague, although his brother had already been convicted of disloyalty, and only the persistent outcry of the press obtained his dismissal after the Government had once refused to yield to public indignation.

Indeed, from the first it has been a constant struggle between the public and the Government or certain powerful interests in the Government. The latter have steadily refused to take the steps necessary to overcome the spy evil until they were forced to it by the people; and even the English people have endured what few other countries would permit. Now and then some public body with sufficient power to make itself heard has acted. School trustees have dismissed their pro-German teachers, and won their cases when the law was appealed to. At least one university rid itself of two or three German professors after the German names attracted public attention. The guardians of a specially fitted hospital refused to accept more German wounded when they found that their entire main building was filled with 1,700 Germans, while in the annex were a thousand British. As the apparatus provided was unexcelled in England, the guardians claimed that its benefits should be more largely open to British wounded.

In all this favouritism to the Germans were bound up the energies of the pacifists and conscientious objectors. In public meetings before their friends, in their own press, in the House of Commons, the most was made by these men of fair treatment to the enemy, their idea of fairness being favouritism. Every month or two a question was asked concerning complaints about the food at the internment camps, although the rations were superior to that which was allowed the British soldier. No complaints seem to have been made at the camps themselves, but there were always friends in the House anxious to forestall rationing. The same influence that rendered the British blockade so ineffective until the United States acted was at work from the beginning of the war to protect the enemy alien in England. While Great Britain was allowing to percolate through its blockade net the very essentials of life in the enemy countries, is was also handing out to German prisoners and to the interned treatment not accorded our own soldiers at home and not expected or asked for our interned in Germany. But the question of the blockade included other issues that hound Great Britain's hands, releasing them only when the United States stood behind it at the source of supplies. What tempers one's sympathy with the difficult position Britain finds herself in in supplying neutral countries is the fact that food was even being shipped to South America.

Yet it is not for Canada to criticize. England's pacifists have never been allowed the freedom of expression enjoyed by a few traitorous spirits in Canada; nor has such political use been made of pro-Germans in England as has characterized political operations in Western Canada. The handling of enemy aliens is theoretically simple of plan and action, but in the everyday life of a nation, even at war, there are interests and influences that seem willing to sacrifice the country to the worst of foes.

The next article of this series will be "The Human Side", describing the marvellous work for the welfare of the distressed in England.

Welfare Work

By Lacey Amy
Part X and Conclusion to 'England in Arms'.
From *The Canadian Magazine,* February 1918.

THE strident of industrial conditions in England during the war might well wonder if Lloyd George has accomplished anything more promising for victory, more beneficial to his country in such a period of stress, than the institution of a new theory in industrial life based on the humanizing of toil. It was away back in the early days of his acceptance by the Empire as the essential cog in the machine of war. At a time when the German was threatening Paris and no obstacle to his victorious march loomed above the horizon, the little Welshman was called by his Premier—but more insistently by his country—to undertake the revolutionizing of warfare in a country whose short-sighted lack of preparation bade fair to be its death sentence.

Guns were needed—more guns—and thousands more. The victorious enemy was not only shattering his way to the capital city of one of the Allies, but he was exacting a toll of the best fighters in the world that threatened quickly to prove his invincibility. The British Tommy, fainting from the fatigue of continued battle, but fighting on without a thought of submission, ground his teeth at his impotence. Man to man he knew his superiority. But man to gun was but fodder. Behind a barrage of murderous shells the German soldier laughed at the puny opposition of a gunless army. The strongest forts known to military science had fallen without a struggle. The direction of the invading army was ever forward. Only when its ammunition failed temporarily was it driven to retreat behind the hills of the Aisne. And then England clamoured for the guns to give the men a chance. Lloyd George the most aggressive politician in sight was given the mission to get them!

Immediately he recognized that the task was not so much a matter of material as of workpeople and factories. And, with his own peculiar foresightedness, he knew that success depended in the final issue on a workpeople contented and able to undertake without more than the minimum of rest the great task of production. To make the munition-makers contented and physically fit for their work more than suitable wages was required. Hours of work must be, for the time

160

subject only to the limits of human endurance. The driving back of the enemy, therefore, hung on the minds and bodies of the workers. And to ensure co-operation of these two allies something in the way of innovation was necessary.

The solution of the problem, as it affected the million women who have thrown themselves into the production of munitions of war, was the creation of a new department in connection with the Ministry of Munitions. As Lloyd George puts it himself: "I had the privilege of setting up something that was known as a welfare department, which was an attempt to take advantage of the present mallability of industry in order to impress upon it more humanitarian conditions, to make labour less squalid and less repellant, more attractive and more healthy." And the results have so far excelled even his hopes that the department is not recognizable to-day by its ambitious creator.

The Welfare Department in Great Britain is assuredly an innovation in industrial life. There has been, and is, a prevailing idea that it is but an English application of a phase of working life already developed in the United States. A Government official modestly deprecated to me any idea of novelty. "You," he said, "know all about it already, of course. For it is not new in America." And he spoke of a certain great factory in the Central States that has for years secured much valuable advertising through its care of its employees. But the difference between any so-called welfare work in America and that developed in Great Britain is sufficient to mark the latter as a distinct creation. Not only is the work differently controlled, but its duties and the direction of its efforts are essentially new.

"Welfare" has been applied in England loosely to everything that introduces a new office dealing directly with the employee of a factory. Jealous and selfish employers have attempted to forestal Government interference by appointing officials whom they dignify with the title of "welfare workers", but whose only duty is to secure larger dividends for the directors. But, strictly speaking, "welfare" in England applies only to the appointees of the Ministry of Munitions; and it is only with these this article will deal. The most dangerous obstacle to the ultimate benefits of real welfare work is the disgust and distrust aroused in the workers by officials who are responsible only to their employers; and there has been more than a suggestion that the Government protect the idea by copyrighting the term it has selected for its appointees.

The welfare worker is a Government employee. The Welfare Department, through a permanent committee, passes on every worker, by interview, by examination of character, record and references. The aim is high, as it necessarily must be to secure a woman whose influence on the munitioneers will be good. Apart from the ordinary qualifications of official position of such authority, she must be educated, dignified, sympathetic, independent, resourceful, diplomatic, physically strong, competent to command, and capable of winning affection as well as respect. It is a large order—so large that the calibre cannot be maintained with any hope of filling the demand. The fact that almost all munition factories are either Government-owned or controlled renders them amenable to the regulation that, with more than a certain number of female employees, one or more welfare workers must be engaged. And the supply is greviously inadequate. It is a feature of English life that caste is another requirement in the welfare workers. Unless the munition workers are sensible of the superior station in life of at least the head of the welfare staff they are reluctant to lend themselves to the relationship imposed by the new idea. Many women, seemingly otherwise fitted to do effective work, have failed to gain the respect so necessary for results. And as the work, if honestly performed, is hard and often discouraging, with long hours and innumerable worries, and with a strain that increases to proportions beyond the reputed strength and competence of woman, even those few who might fill the position with success hesitate before assuming the tremendous responsibilities.

The true welfare official is selected by the Welfare Department of the Ministry of Munitions, accordingly, and approved of by the management of the factory where her work is to be. As a Government employee she is independent, save in employment and discharge, of the management. Her position might appear anomalous and impossible, but in reality, owing to the wonderful results that have appeared, the munition firms have accepted the relationship with a grace that grows to appreciation. As a Government official it is her duty in general to see that the working conditions are reasonable and fair, that the factory equipment is sanitary and safe, that dismissals are only for good cause, that the moral atmosphere is satisfactory, that the girls are paid according to established rates; in short, that every surrounding of the female worker is suitable to her sex, her physical and moral requirements, and to her protection. The value of the welfare worker to the management appears in her ability to settle disputes, maintain discipline, raise the morale of the girls, secure from them a full co-operation in production and in factory interest, and protect the firm from the expense and loss of time arising from a wrong mental attitude and from accident.

The technical titles applied to the workers are somewhat descriptive. The head may be a "supervisor" or a "superintendent". The former works without assistants in the smaller factories. The superintendent has directly under her a staff of welfare assistants and auxiliary forces. Properly speaking, only her assistants who have been approved of by the Department are "welfare workers", but a superintendent is usually considered competent to select assistants who would satisfy the Department.

The duties of the superintendent are too multifarious to be described save under the general term "welfare". Obviously there is little she can do which has not some connection with the interests of her women munition-workers. Outside the general authority secured to her by her official appointment, her powers rest with the factory management. If the latter is sympathetic and satisfied with her, she is sometimes given almost unlimited authority over the women in the shops. The one Canadian welfare superintendent in Great Britain, with the fullest recognition by both Government and factory officials, has practically supreme control over every woman in the factory area, munition-workers and office staff. In her rests authority to select and dismiss employees, to pass on the dismissals by the foreman, to promulgate regulations of any kind affecting female labour. As head of the Labour Bureau every new employee must conform to the ideals she has established. The requirements in this department alone, of 3,500 women workers, with the ordinary changes of industrial life and the extraordinary and unexpected demands of war conditions, is difficult to imagine. Lavatory, hospital and rest-room accommodation is directly subject to her. She is one of a committee of three to manage a canteen for 5,000 employees. She has charge of the cleaning staffs. Her orders in the business office are obeyed as the manager's. Female employees obtain from her leave to pass from the building during working hours and to remain from work for special reasons.

But these are the mere outlines of her general work, the listed duties. They are, in reality, the least of her real welfare work. Her main care is to secure the confidence of her girls, to convince them that in her they have a friend. She protects them from the momentary exasperation of worried foremen. Every possible convenience and comfort she obtains for them. Rest-rooms and canteen and lavatories, floors and windows of shops are kept under her eye for cleanliness and fittings. A girl on work too strenuous for her strength is transferred by her to easier duties. Petty thieving is controlled by the firm's police under her direction. Complaints of every kind are brought to her for settlement, from a badly cooked meal at the canteen to the partiality of a charge hand. She orders improvements to ventilation, heating and lighting, and sees that the girls who have leisure to sit are provided with seats. She inquires into mistakes in pay envelopes and advises the management on inadequate rates.

And still the list is incomplete. She arbitrates disagreements, not only between the foremen and the girls, but between the girls themselves. She moves, when conditions warrant it, girls into more congenial shops. She directs them to the firm's hospitals in case of sickness. She takes the children of mothers who must work for a living and finds them good homes. She firmly dismisses girls physically unfitted for their duties, but offers them re-employment when their health warrants it. She keeps in touch with every sick employee, sending her assistants to their homes to inquire their wants. She supervises the boarding-houses of the workers and to some extent their homes. She encourages them to come to her in all the petty troubles of life, whether in connection with their work or not.

While her office doors are frequently closed, by stress of work, to the factory officials, they are always open to the girls. To be a mother to them is the highest aim and the most productive of the right kind of welfare superintendent.

This intimate and authoritative contact with her girls is not maintained at the cost of discipline. Indeed, the welfare superintendent is the source of discipline as well as of protection and comfort. In every move she considers the rights and wishes of the foremen. Leave is given—except for compulsory reasons—only as the demands of the shop permit. The foreman's authority is sustained in every reasonable instance. His work is lightened by the application of discipline by one who understands conditions and sympathizes with his difficulties in applying his authority to a new class of worker whom he does not quite understand and is too busy to study.

The course of an ordinary forenoon's work is revealing.

1. Arriving at 8.30, she examines the reports left by her night assistants, nurses, women police and forewomen of the cleaners.

2. Letters opened and answered.

3. Twenty new girls engaged.

4. Special committee meeting on air raid protection.

5. Trouble at the canteen made the dismissal of the night cook necessary, after which application for a new one had to be made to the Government Labour Exchange.

6. Discharge granted to woman physically unfit—a case to be followed up. Explanation made to foreman and superintendent of the branch of the factory in which she worked.

7. Girl released from one shop through lack of work is found a place in another.

8. Girl ordered off night work by her doctor is exchanged to day work with another girl.

9. Foreman came to explain absence of one of his girls. Arrangements made to get her pay to her.

10. Girl came to complain of her discharge by foreman. Latter spoken to over telephone and found to be at fault, and girl found work in another shop.

11. Made out orders for several pairs of overalls for girls.

12. Two girls came to complain of treatment of another girl in same shop. Note made to inquire into it.

13. Underforeman inquired how to enforce discipline among his workers. As many complaints of his severity had come in, a friendly and satisfactory talk resulted.

14. Injured girl reported no insurance received. Gave orders to have it looked into.

15. Girl absent the day before without leave or excuse was warned.

16. Sergeant at gate came for instructions about passes out.

17. Put through order for ambulance-room supplies.

18. Assistant reports.

19. Two women discharged on the previous day came to express their thanks for her kindness in paving the way to other work. One brought her baby for inspection.

20. Five minutes' talk with the manager.

21. In a hasty run through one of the shops discovered girl with sore throat. Sent her immediately to the nurse.

22. Girl injured a few days before came to say her doctor said she might return to work in a week.

23. Glanced over time sheets and sent assistant to inquire reasons of absentees; also to get report on mistake in a girl's pay.

In addition there were hasty telephone conversations with a dozen foremen. Every afternoon much of the time is spent in the shops with the girls, watching them work, studying conditions, inspecting the efficiency of the charge hands, etc. Government officials must be seen and visitors entertained, purchases made and plans developed.

For the welfare work which is outside the strict limits of business the firm provides her with a fund. It is perhaps the best proof of the growth of the welfare idea. Old employees who cannot afford the expense of illness are assisted. Others with unexpected temporary strains on their resources may borrow and repay at their leisure. Even those necessarily dismissed by the fluctuations of production are assisted until they obtain new situations. And the welfare superintendent with her heart in her work is too apt to forget her own pocket and expend a great part of her salary in this kind of help. Now the idea has spread to the male employees, whose wives and families profit from the fund.

To assist her in these never-ending duties this welfare superintendent has a staff of sufficient proportions to relieve her of what portion may be left to other shoulders; but the intimate relationship with the girls cannot be dismissed by any amount of assistance. Her private secretary is her immediate representative. Three assistant welfare workers see that her instructions are carried out, represent her at night, and visit the sick and absent. A Labour Bureau assistant first culls out the applicants for work. Three trained nurses are on constant duty for accident or sudden sickness, making their reports to her and subject to her instructions. Three policewomen see to the direct enforcement of her regulations, reporting to her and recognizing her authority, although appointed (subject to her approval) by the Government organization of policewomen. There are, in addition, clerks and office boys who do not properly enter into the welfare work. Her supreme authority is recognized by the title of "lady superintendent", every detail of the management of female labour being handed over to her by the manager.

The factory equipment coming specially within her sphere is the last word in welfare work. Through a sympathetic management every provision has been made for the comfort of the women. Two large rest-rooms are always open to those temporarily idle through accident to the machines or illness. The rooms are bright and airy, fitted with easy-chairs, sofas, tables and reading material. There are two hospitals or "ambulance rooms" equipped with every modern requirement, with beds and other necessities and presided over by trained nurses whose services are at the disposal of the patients until recovery. A private ambulance is kept for rushing serious cases to the hospital or home The canteen is one of the provisions of war which will continue into peace if it is found to pay. During the war most firms are content to lose—sometimes as much as a thousand dollars a week—for the immediate profit in other respects from this feature of welfare work. Long hours, fewer holidays and the unusual strains consequent upon the war make it doubly necessary that special provision be made to fit the munition-maker for the unending needs of the armies; and the woman worker, unaccustomed to the demands upon her strength, is more susceptible to the limitations of her methods of life. Under the welfare worker these girls have been induced to govern their meals by the requirements of their bodies, not by the custom of their class or the momentary taste of their palates. Pudding and cake have given place to meat, and the canteen meal is the main one of the day. Never in their lives have the working classes of England been offered such meals as are served them so cheaply in the canteens. Never again will they be willing to return to the former comfortless, insufficient fare of pre-war days. It is a welfare work that in itself justifies the new industrial department.

In explosive factories the duties of the welfare worker are directed more towards the health and protection of the girls, one great difficulty in the employment of female labour on explosives being their slowness to realize the danger of disobeying regulations. The welfare worker impresses the necessity upon them and protects them from their own carelessness.

There are features of welfare work which have received much greater fame than those outlined above, but only because they are more unusual and spectacular. Organized dances, dramatic clubs, swimming and other classes, entertainment of various kinds—these are the novelties of welfare work which have been pictured in the papers. But they are really only the frills. The welfare worker with time and strength to throw herself into such extraneous luxuries must be neglecting the more intimate and effective side of her work. Provide a girl with healthy surroundings, a clean moral atmosphere, sustaining food, sufficient rest, protection from tyranny and injustice, and a human heart to seek for advice, and her relaxation is not apt to go far astray. The original idea of welfare work, as practised, was amusement. It has altered to personal care and sympathy. The earlier form of welfare worker is finding a more congenial sphere in organizing bazaars and entertaining the soldiers. The new worker does not neglect entertainment, but she has discovered how little it serves to secure the hold she desires.

In the search for judicious welfare workers England is handicapped by the prevalence of caste. While it is for the present necessary, owing to the peculiarities of English life, that the welfare superintendent be obviously of a higher social standing, the granite walls between the classes in England are too high to permit of the fraternity and unsullied sympathy that must exist between munition worker and welfare worker, except in cases all too few. And the fault is as much of the working people as of the women who have offered themselves for this grand work of industrial improvement.

The welfare idea would be abortive, especially in time of war, did it not express itself in terms of efficiency and production. It is in increased output, as well as in its moral effect, that it faces the opposition of labour agitators who see in it the lessening of their influence for evil. It requires little insight into psychology to appreciate that the contended, healthy worker, whose moral sense is cultivated, is the most productive. The aim of the welfare worker is best tested by the results of the improvements she has introduced; and concerning that there is no question. So emphatic is the average employer in his praise of the new idea that hundreds of them have expressed their determination to continue it after the war. Strikes among the girls are almost unknown. Discipline is simple. Idling is infinitely less than among the men—especially than among the young men who have found in munition factories their exemption from the trenches. The discipline of the welfare worker is an appeal to the girl's moral sense rather than to force.

And the girls are proving the richness of the soil in which the new idea is spreading seed. The old frivolous conception of munition-making as the means to a gay, extravagant life of pleasure is passing.

The girl who once put her money in a new hat every fortnight and a pair of boots a month now probably lends it to her country for the winning of the war. Her nights, that used to be occupied in cinema or dance halls or street loafing, are spent in sewing and profitable entertainment. "We never knew there were women in the world like you" is the cry of their souls to the new sort of woman who has come into their lives.

Less sentimental and appealing, perhaps, may be the revolution the successful welfare worker is introducing into industrial relationship. Her consideration for the foremen is engendering a new spirit in the workshops. Co-operation is taking the place of petty jealousies. What was once a medley of shops is now one combined factory. The focus of the female labour of the factory in the one head is encouraging a similar desire among the men. And when shop works with shop the result to Great Britain in the rivalry of peace times cannot be overestimated. With this new spirit of co-operation must arise a new relationship between capital and labour. It is in this rests the future of the industrial and commercial life of Great Britain.

From an older post and research: "...Graduating in 1899, he married as his first wife Lillian Eva Payne. Mrs. Amy was a personality in her own right. During World War I, she was the first Canadian woman ever to be made a Member of the Order of the British Empire, an honour awarded to her in connection with her work with the Massey-Harris Hospital at Dulwich and later as Lady Superintendent of one of the largest munitions factories in England, where she was in charge of more than 3,000 women." /drf

23rd February, 2001

Reference: 45/16/01

Dear Madam,

Thank you for your letter dated 12th February in which you requested information in connection with an award to Mrs. Lillian Eva Amy, MBE.

Having searched our records with the information provided I have found the following details.

Set out below is an extract taken from the London Gazette dated 3rd June 1918:

CENTRAL CHANCERY OF THE ORDERS OF KNIGHTHOOD

St. James's Palace S.W.1

The KING has been graciously pleased, on the occasion of the Celebration of His Majesty's Birthday, to make the following promotions in, and appointments to, the Most Excellent Order of the British Empire for services in connection with the War:

To be a Member of the Civil Division of the said Most Excellent Order:
Mrs. Lillian Eva Amy, Welfare Supervisor, Messrs. C. A. Vandervell & Co.

Mrs. Amy received her MBE from His Majesty King George V at Buckingham Palace on 24th September 1918.

This is the only information I have regarding the above and I do hope that it has been of some assistance to you.

Yours sincerely,

Alexander de Montfort

Jean Pickard,
5-312-4 Street,
Brandon,
Manitoba
R7A 3G9
170   CANADA

After Three Years

By Lacey Amy
Part XI. of England in Arms
From *The Canadian Magazine*, March 1918.

SINCE this series of articles began so much has happened within their scope that anything approaching a complete examination of the measures taken in the British Isles to cope with war conditions must include those adopted after the trying experiences of three years of war. It would be reasonable to expect that in such a period of unprecedented struggle for existence the problem of the nation would be solved in so far as organization and experience could solve them, that the difficulties still remaining would be not in effective planning or decision but solely in the strain and deprivations rendered necessary by a powerful foe. Yet only the blindest fatuity could assert that England has solved the simplest of her war problems only the most superficial student would declare that even the obviously wise and fair measures have been taken.

The status of the women has been growing stronger every day. More and more they have been offering themselves for the needs of the war and more and more they have proved themselves the real backbone of production. It is only due their earnest participation in munition making to admit that they perform their work more carefully and quickly than the same number of men. They have been set by the thousand at tasks hitherto considered beyond their capacity, in strength and brains, and in not one case that has come within my knowledge have they failed to exceed the production of the men in a very few weeks. The reason is not that they are more able, but that they throw more vim and enthusiasm into it. They are not too busy haggling over privileges to remember that the soldiers at the Front are looking to them for the shells and the guns. The women have saved the Empire, though there are hundreds of thousands of the better classes doing their utmost, by idling and extravagance, to depreciate the sum total. More than a million and a quarter women were engaged on the first of September, 1917, on work formerly done by men. In government factories and in the Civil Service they have released a quarter of a million men. In Government controlled factories half a million of them have found employment, and in commerce generally more than three hundred thousand more. In these two branches of service they have released three-quarters of a million men.

All told, there are more than four and a half million women and girls in classified employment, not including domestic servants, hospital workers, and those employed in small shops.

Their interests have been studied by the Ministry of Munitions, and after tests the standard number of hours of employment has been reduced to forty-eight a week with increase of output; and during the year two raises in wages have been officially declared. So important a part do they play in the necessary war production that a special committee has been appointed to deal with their wages, hours of labour, and conditions of employment.

The latest call for their services has come from the military organization in France. The first lot of ten thousand, for office and mess duties hitherto performed by men, was overwhelmingly supplied, and during the latter half of 1917 the demand was continuous. So insatiable was it, and so eager were girls to undertake this new work, that the drain on the munition factories in England was seriously felt, the type of worker finding favour in France being the same as that sought for the factories. Now the Admiralty has appealed for women to relieve naval ratings on shore duty. Were all England imbued with the spirit of its average woman the war would be further advanced towards victory than it is to-day.

The problem in the case of female labour is the after-war results. Certainly thousands of women, having tasted the pleasures of earning and of steady employment, will be unwilling to return to idleness. It is the knowledge of this that has interfered with their acceptance in the councils of labour. From the first, labour unions demanded that pre-war conditions be restored immediately with peace, and as a further block to the ingress of women into industrial competition, the same wage was demanded for both sexes. The women accepted the wage at first with eagerness, but a few of the leaders quickly discovered the reason and are now insisting on an equality that is not absolute but based on the differences in strength, sex, and the requirements of physical well-being. For, while the women have a better record of production than the men, it is telling on their health and nerves, and without the incentive of war it is certain that their production will decrease.

The position of the farmer has steadily improved. But it cannot be said, unfortunately, that he has done much to warrant it. While the farmer in England was, for many years before the war, in the lowest plane of society and the least profitable, his rise to a deserved recognition as the solution of the food problem of an island kingdom has had a natural result. Filled with the idea of his unwonted importance to the country and to victory, and thrilled with his new power, he has ignored the demand for a common sacrifice and refuses to direct his efforts to production that does not bring him returns consistent with the level established by the needs of a country short of all food stuffs. He insists that his every acre be guaranteed by a Government driven to extremity for supplies, otherwise he reserves the right to confine his crops to the profitable grains and roots, or to leave it idle. If he is asked to grow potatoes he must be protected in a profit beyond his wildest dreams of former years. If the profits of barley, for instance, are eliminated by decreased liquor production, he must see the loss made up from another source or threats of lessened production are issued.

And therein the farmer is but requiting for the hardship of his lot before the war. Yet, great as are his profits to-day, he resists the extension of the higher returns to his workmen. Three dollars a week was the offer of a farmer for a man to work from 5.30 a.m., to 9.00 p.m., and from that the man must board and lodge himself. Even the Government established a rate of $1.50 a week above their billets for girl plum pickers on the farms, railway fares to be paid by the workers. Girls on the land were paid three dollars a week, supplying their own food.

The Education Bill, introduced by the President of the Board of Education as a remedy for the glaring evils in the education system of Great Britain, has been received by the people with the loudest acclaim—and quietly shelved by the authorities. There was too much innovation in it for those with power to accept it without serious misgivings. Oxford University has led the fight against it, not openly but none the less effectively. For Oxford University represents education as it has been for centuries in England. It eschews science, clings to classics as the soul of England, and resents the claim of anyone else to criticize or advise on education.

The result is that the Bill, to the middle of December, 1917, has not even been considered in the House. Public bodies have protested. The new papers have made demands. But those subtle muscles which wield the power of Great Britain from behind the scenes have intervened. The Bill was at first refused consideration in the last session of 1917. It was soberly contended by Bonar Law three months before the end of the session, that there would be no time for discussing the Bill, although time was always found readily enough for inconsequential subjects, and hours every day were wasted on questions and answers which should have been deleted for the good of the country. It was obvious that the majority of the Government were against the Bill of the Minister. But the demand grew so insistent that finally the hope was expressed of completing one reading, leaving the final stages to another session. At the time of writing, there it stands, the end depending upon whether the balance of power rests with the people or with the forces for conservatism. It takes more than three years of war to break the grip of tradition in England.

The liquor question has resolved itself into a typical capitulation on the part of the Government. That started as an apparent effort to conserve food stuffs for a more or less suffering country by directing grains from beer to bread, has become merely another official failure to live up to promises—or threats. After announcing drastic curtailment of the consumption of food stuffs in the manufacture of beer, the Government yielded to pressure, largely artificial and concentrated, and increased the quantity one-third at the middle of 1917. During the year ending September, 1916, there were 65,000,000 bushels of grain and 160,000 tons of sugar used for the manufacture of liquor. During 1917 the quantity permitted was more than half that amount. When it is considered that sugar is absolutely unobtainable by a great part of the people of England, and the ration is set at half a pound a week, this amount assumes considerable importance. The Government's excuse that the sugar thus consumed is largely unfit for human consumption is misleading, for not only is much of it exactly what is used on the table, but its importation into England takes the same space in the limited shipping as the same quantity of edible sugar for general distribution.

The cause of the Government's surrender was a well-organized campaign by the newspapers and brewers. One or two of the largest London papers published each day reports of serious disturbances throughout the country through the shortage of beer, and although some of these were entirely without foundation, the workers of England were convinced that beer was a vital necessity and that strikes were expected of them.

To meet the demand with the least expenditure of foodstuffs the Government authorized a weaker quality, termed government beer, and to it thereafter was accredited by every "drunk" the cause of his downfall. Being a government brand, the magistrates could scarcely convict. But the main result of the new liquor restrictions was an increased profit for brewer and retailer. The annual returns of the breweries show that they never made such profits; and the retailer, working less than half the prewar hours, asked what he wished for his stock. So independent did he become that there were saloons in London showing signs prohibiting the entrance of women, an unusual sex distinction. At last the Government was forced to intervene and establish prices. But the Government scale of prices, in the experience of this war, protects the merchants in a percentage of profit on which he can afford to smile benevolently.

In the meantime government purchase has advanced no further. The report of the Commission appointed to investigate is against purchase, and everyone seems content to leave it at that as a plan too radical to adopt without several years of deliberation.

The fondest admirers of the war government of Great Britain must admit that the methods of handling labour, man-power, food, and the enemy alien have savored little of real war. Great Britain labours under a number of special disqualifications. These might be summed up as excessive deliberation and delay, class distinctions, unpardonable tolerance, and conventionalism. And the last includes all the others. Somewhere in this short list might be found the foundation of every obstacle to victory. Lack of decision and firmness, of organizing ability, and excess of pride are other descriptions of the country's deficiencies.

Inexperience in organization, where a country has succeeded fairly well on the plan laid down by former generations, has exhibited itself in almost every move since the war began. Today it is evident in the internecine strife among the Government departments. It is plain in the food muddle, which is to-day in a more chaotic state than ever. It is to be seen in the labour troubles, the record of the navy, the shortage of man-power at the Front, and of production in England.

The position of labour offers the most serious trouble. Asquith's foolish promise of exemption to twenty-nine unions is an instance of the weakness of a war government in the national extremity.

Irrespective of any crisis, these unions insist on adherence to the promise, and the blame is not so much with them as with the Cabinet that had a country on its shoulders. Union labour has not changed its opinion noticeably since it lent itself to conscription under certain conditions, but union labour, as governed by its main executives, is almost a negligible power now, partly from its own thoughtlessness, partly from governmental weakness. The Engineers' disloyal strike in May, 1917, brought to the fore a power that has been robbing the executives of their authority. The Engineers struck for nothing but fear of being taken into the army. Whatever other excuse may have been given, determination not to serve with the colours was the real one. They had no complaint, but new orders for obtaining the necessary additional soldiers by extending the dilution of labour gave them a pretext for calling a strike. And they won. The Government rescinded everything, although it had the country behind it and could have taught a much needed lesson in patriotism that would have solved for the duration of the war every difficulty of man-power. Were the workers convinced that the penalty of loafing was fighting in France two-thirds their number would produce what they are now producing, and there would be no thought of strikes.

Having obtained almost all they wished, the engineers resumed work; and for a time there was comparative peace. But during the last two months of 1917 the labour situation was a boiling disturbance. The South Wales miners frankly took a vote to decide whether they would resist the Government in combing out the new men introduced into the mines since the war began. The Coventry aeroplane makers, engaged in the most vital of munition production, walked out and remained idle a week until they, too won all they asked. All over England were demands for higher wages, shorter hours, greater privileges, and the reinstatement of employees dismissed for the most outrageous offences.

The reason for the ferment was easy to find. The Government lacked back bone—simply that. The submission to the engineers, although the whole country was so strong against them that at the end they were but looking for an excuse to return to the shops and feared to wear their union badges, paved the way to every strike that has occurred since. Winston Churchill, already convicted of incapacity by an official commission, was appointed Minister of Munitions purely as a political expedient. And Churchill's first few months in office seemed to justify his selection. Never had there been so few strikes. But suddenly they blazed forth all over the country, so seriously as to jeopardize the war in 1918. And the secret was out when, without consulting those directly affected, he declared a general increase of pay for the engineers. Immediately other unions struck for increases and other advantages. It was found that railwaymen had long suffered from a ridiculous discrepancy between their wages and those of even the unskilled in other trades which had ignored the war and thought only of self. It was found, too, that the increase so lightly granted affected a score of trades not contemplated.

The temporary immunity from strikes had been because every demand had been met. The unpardonable extent to which this weakness went may be illustrated by one example. When a shop steward was caught making tools for himself from Government material (it was a government controlled factory) in government time and promptly dismissed, a strike was declared for his reinstatement. And the Government forced the firm to submit. Besides the principle involved, it is natural that ever since then the reinstated employee has been a cause of constant trouble and agitation. Such folly was rampant all over England. The natural result was that strikes were called on the flimsiest pretexts. The men jeeringly declaring that the Government was afraid of them.

But this was not union labour as constituted before the war. Every strike has been engineered by the shop-stewards, a new force that has crept in since the factories were filled with able-bodied young men whose only concern is to escape service in France. The regular union executives and power of unionism to-day is in the hands of those young shirkers who do not hesitate to declare their reasons for working on munitions. Unionism thought to protect itself by forcing all workers to join. In reality it lost every shred of power by the act. To-day every local union is a law unto itself. The Coventry strike was called by the shop stewards against the union leaders' instructions, just as the engineers' had been. And the only bone of contention was the recognition of the shop stewards.

Wrapped in this question of labour is the other of obtaining men for the trenches. Anyone who knows conditions in the factories of England is aware that hundreds of thousands of fit young men could be cleared out with profit to production, even though they were not put in khaki. The majority of these are doing as little as possible, they are always on the watch for grounds for striking, they interfere with those who would produce to their utmost, they refuse to permit the women to be taught certain operations well within their capacity, and they are almost all recruits to this kind of work since 1914. Yet the only apparent concern of the Government seems to be to assure them of exemption. And since more soldiers are an absolute essential, raising the age to 45 is being seriously considered while these young slackers loaf in security. It is a fact that experienced factory hands discharged from the army have been called up again from the munition factories while these young fellows look on from the next benches and laugh. It is also a fact that married men with large families, men too old for the hard life of the Front, others whose businesses will close with their conscription, are relentlessly put into khaki to fight for these strong youths without dependants or extra bills of expense to present to the Government.

Every government department seems to delight in refusing to release its youthful clerks for service. Each being king in its own realm and jealously guarding its power, there is none with authority to comb them out, although battalions could be replaced by girls and older men. It continues, too, to be a department habit to order tribunals to exempt applicants for no reasonable excuse. And England is teeming with non-combatant young men wearing the red tab of headquarters or the khaki of soft jobs far from the sound of war. It is not lack of men that keeps the army in want.

The food problem is too wide to be more than touched here. There is no daylight showing, even after almost a year of submarine war. Hundreds of orders have been issued by the Food Controller, thousands of appeals. But they have affected little save to establish prices at an unjustifiable level, force the poor to stand in queues hours of every day, and reserve to the merchant an exhorbitant profit. The House of Commons is made up of men interested in trade—one would know it without acquaintance with the members. It may safely be said that not a single law observes the good of the people at the expense to the merchant. Merchants are making more money than they ever dreamed of. The country is bringing in the food stuffs and handing them over to the stores for extreme profits. And when a law threatens to interfere, the merchants ignore it with impunity. Laws that appear every few days in public print are openly flouted, and to protest is to be denied supplies. Every time a maximum price is established by regulation it instantly becomes the minimum price as well. Now and then a merchant in some distant village or in the East End of London is proceeded against, and the papers are so filled with threats that few read them.

The attempt to regulate prices and supplies have demonstrated the inability of the authorities to organize and devise reasonable methods. Only those of the lower classes who have time to stand in queues can obtain supplies. Thus the hard-working munition makers find themselves short half the week. England's short stocks seem to be reserved for the idle, and no attempt has yet been made to change it. Take sugar as an example of muddling. Although the rationing of sugar was determined on more than six months before it was put into force, the plan had to be completely altered during that six months, after the first scheme had been issued and everyone had done his part in the registration, and for reasons that were obviously insuperable defects from the start. It is also an instance of the wasted and misdirected zeal of officialdom that the postal customs filched two pounds of sugar from a small gift sent from Canada to a Canadian war worker in England, and at the same time, on the Government's own figures, 8,000 tons a week were being issued above the rations without any effort to trace them.

A half dozen food commodities have been short, not so much because they were not in the stores but from unfair and unequal distribution. In every commodity in which the demand seems to exceed the supply there has been a riot of mismanagement and unfairness. The last month of 1917 saw an insistent demand for rationing all round, to prevent queues and to ensure something resembling even distribution. If there was one thing in the situation that was threatening unrest it was the manner in which the food question was handled.

The shortage of other commodities has been equally mismanaged. Petrol affords an illuminating example. Given over finally into the hands of a pool formed of the importers themselves, it travelled upwards in price until a government investigation was demanded, when it immediately dropped several cents a gallon. The Government's later efforts to control its use have driven many cars from the streets, but more by threat than by force. Petrol may still be used for domestic business, for business purposes, for going to and from the station, and for everything connected with war work. The loopholes were innumerable. So long as a man is in khaki no questions are asked. Business men have their cars for running to the office, actors have licences at their pleasure, but, worst of all, the taxi is practically unrestricted. For the Lord Mayor's banquet orders were given that anyone might use his car.

Now and then the law bestirs itself in a characteristic manner. A taxi driver was fined $250 for carrying a government official and his wife many miles into the country to bury their pet dog in a dog cemetery—but nothing was done to the official. A poor street match vendor was fined for overcharging for a box of matches— but a hundred stores were at the same time openly doing the same, and other laws were being broken. A Canadian General's mother was summoned for using petrol to attend church—but she might have hired a taxi to take her to a restaurant and have kept its engine running during the meal. Two women were fined for engaging a car that was not a taxi to take them to the theatre—but had the garage keeper sent a taxi nothing could have been done to them.

It is such inconsistencies that bring the authorities and their methods into disrepute, until one wonders how much it takes at home to discount the country's best efforts in the field.

A similar indecision and fatuousness exists in the treatment of alien enemies. There is no reason why Germany should not be kept informed of all that England contemplates, if freedom of German-born means espionage and all the world knows by this time that it does. Scores of influential Germans continue to be granted freedom and other favours, each backed by prominent politicians or titled people. When Laszlo, a popular Austrian painter, proved by a letter three years ago to be an Austrian at heart—when he was brought before a court of inquiry for internment, several of England's most prominent men protested against locking him away; and because they were of the upper classes the Government refused to divulge their names. There is a large fund collected in England for the dependants of interned Germans, Cadburys, of cocoa fame, being the main supporters. And the wives of these interned Germans are already granted an allowance higher than the wives of the British soldiers used to get. The interned ones, too, were given more liberal allowances of food than are prescribed for the British people. The brother of the German Governor who murdered Nurse Cavell, interned in England, was allowed to enter a nursing home on the plea of ill-health. An army officer, once Krupp's agent in London, ordered out of France as a suspicious person, although with the British forces, was immediately taken on the British Intelligence Department where military secrets are the only commodity dealt in. These instances of extreme tolerance and folly might be multiplied over and over again.

For almost two years I have studied Britain's methods at home for making war. I have made every allowance for tradition, for excusable conditions. I have looked through the eyes of an Imperialist. But in the end I can see an early end to the war only by more aggressive and sensible methods. England does not make war with both fists—that is the trouble.

John Shiwak, of Labrador, the only Eskimo soldier to lay down his life for the Empire.
Photo. by J. Cook.

An Eskimo Patriot

By Lacey Amy
From *The Canadian Magazine*, July 1918.

Images are from various sources

THE grief of it is keener to me to-day than it was a week ago when the news first reached me; and I know the shadows of time will never hide it, though tingeing the grief to a brighter hue in a great pride at having known him, at having been called by him one of his two friends in England during his trying days in khaki.

To know John Shiwak, even in the old days of peace, was to be filled with a mysterious admiration that grew without realizing its own roots, a quiet fondness that complimented one's self-respect. But to have been in touch with him even by mail at the end, to have heard from his lips, in words only a few hours old, the unfaltering admiration of him, was to be branded with a mark time dare not try to obliterate. And to have seen him in the moment of his passage! But John's story must be told first—and I hope that ten thousand slackers may read it and see the picture as I see it—which is infinitely better than I am able to present it.

It was in the summer of 1911 that I met John. It was *only* in that summer that I met him. But to have met him once was to remember him always. Seeking new out-of-the-world places in or around Canada, I had picked on the bleak coast of Labrador. Across the straits from North Sydney the boat had plunged through a parallel swell all night, and in the morning landed us at Point aux Basques. Twenty-six hours of travel on a narrow-gauge railway, through hours on end of manless land, had brought us to St. John's, that inimitably quaint capital of Newfoundland.

And one afternoon we pushed our way through the heaped boxes of cod and salt and general merchandise that line St. John's piers and boarded a little mail steamer that ran twice a month—seldom more than five times a year—"down" the semi-settled coast of Newfoundland for five hundred miles, and then another five hundred far off to the north, into the birthplace of the iceberg, along the uncharted, barren, rugged shores of a country God never intended man to inhabit—Labrador.

"The battalion still argue which was the first to reach the bridge, John or another. But John reached the height of the little arch and turned to wave his companions on."

Yet it was a pleasant trip, one to look back upon with no shuddering memories, but with a dreamy halo of unreality dimming its thousand unwonted events and sights, a composite picture that frays off about the edges and centres about one lone figure—John

Shiwak, the Eskimo.

We were a motley crowd on board. For the next two weeks we would be bound to each other in the depressions and exaltations, the trials and strains of a confined existence that centred and circled and spread no farther than the tight dining-room and the after-deck. My personal variation was visits to the bridge, where I spent days at a time. The transient passenger list consisted of the woman-who-worries and myself, three professional world-vagrants who travelled as most people work, a mysterious newly-married couple whom none knew better at the end than at the beginning. And below decks crowded a score of Newfoundland fishermen and fish merchants on their way to the great cod grounds along the Labrador.

And there was John.

I was aware of him at first as he sat at the Newfoundlanders' table in the dining saloon, never uttering a word, watching with both eyes every movement at the table of the "foreigners". Presently I noted that he ceased to spread his bread on his hand, that he gave up his knife except for its legitimate purposes, that he stopped reaching as the others at his table did. Frequently I caught his eye, and always it dropped in confusion—only to return in a minute to the ways of our table. In a couple of days he was eating in the manner of so-called culture.

I watched for him on deck, but for several days caught only fleeting glimpses of him. And always he was the daintiest man on board. Evidently he had invested in a new wardrobe in St. John's, and the muscular, short, straight-standing figure of him did each garment fullest justice. Twice a day he appeared in different array—in the mornings usually in knickers and sealskin moccasins.

Not a word did I ever see him speak to another. He would appear on deck for a half-hour twice a day, lean over the railing within sound of our voices, and disappear as silently as he came. I set myself the task of intruding on his reticence, of breaking his silence. In truth it was a task. Observing him one day watching the unloading of salt into the small boats that play the part of wharves on the Labrador coast, I leaned on the railing beside him and made some trivial inquiry about the scene of bustle. His reply was three words. To my second question, after several minutes, the reply was two words. And then he turned away. It was discouraging. But soon thereafter I noticed that when I stopped to look over the rail, if it were not in too quiet a part of the ship, John was leaning just far enough away to be out of range of questions. I took to wandering about, stopping by myself to look out on the sights of shore and iceberg. The interval between us decreased.

Then one night we stopped, in the sudden darkness that falls in that quarter shortly after ten of an August evening, to pick up a missionary and his wife and household goods. It was a task of hours, for everything had to be brought out to the steamer in one small rowboat. I was looking down from the forward deck on the twinkling lights below, hearing the oaths of busy seamen, in my ears the creaking of the steam winch. Suddenly there broke on the night from the outer darkness the shuddering howl of a wolf, then a chorus of howls. I raised myself to listen, peering out into the darkness of the sea where there were only scores of tiny islands, and beyond, scores of towering icebergs.

"The Labrador band," explained a quiet voice beside me, modest to the verge of self-deprecation, but with a twinkle in it somewhere.

It was John Shiwak. And the ice was broken. I soothed his obvious nervousness by keeping to the text for the moment. "The Labrador band" is the term applied to the howling huskies, most of whom are set down on islands during their summer months of uselessness that they might be out of the way.

Far into the morning John and I sat up there in the dirty, deserted bow, as the ship felt its way through the islands on its northward crawl. By the pitch of the boat we knew when the islands ceased to screen us from the swell outside. Now and then an icy breath registered the passing of an iceberg; and once a disturbing crackling far outside, and a great plunge, told of a Greenland monster that had yielded at last to the wear of sun and wave. Not a sound of life broke the northern silence save the quiet voice of the captain on the bridge above, and the weird howls of hungry or disturbed huskies only one stage removed from their wolfish origin. And in those hours I learned much of John Shiwak's immediate history.

He was a hunter in the far interior by winter, a handiman in his district by summer. The past winter had been a good one for him—a silver fox skin, for instance, which he had disposed of to the Hudson's Bay Company for four hundred and sixty-nine dollars. And on the strength of such unusual profits he had gone down to St. John's, Newfoundland, whence all good things come to Labrador—and whither all good and bad things go from Labrador—and had plunged into the one great time of his life. His memory of that two weeks of civilization congealed into a determination to repeat the visit each summer. And I know that the dissipations of a great and strange city had had nothing to do with its attractions.

In his conversation there was the solemnity of a man who does much thinking in vast silences. Everything was presented to me in the vivid succinctness that delights the heart of an editor. John's life had been filled with the essentials. So was his comment on life. When we parted for our berths I was conscious of a series of pictures that lacked no necessary touch of a master hand; but repetition in the stilted language and phrasing of civilization was impossible. The wonderful gift of nature was John's, and the marvel of it grew on me through the night hours.

Next morning I smiled at him from our table, and some new life in his eyes convinced me the recognition was not unwelcome. And when we few wanderers collected as usual on the after-deck, there was John a few yards away leaning on the rail. I went to him, taking the woman-who-worries, and after a few monosyllabic words he took advantage of our interest in some scene on shore to glide away. But an hour later he was there again and thereafter he adopted us as his friends. For the next two days we separated only for meals and sleep. And on the night of the second day, as we swung a little into the open to make the Hamilton Inlet, a storm arose. And through the storm a tiny rowboat bobbed up to us in the moonlight, poised for minutes in the flush of a great danger as it struggled to reach us without crushing against our sides, and then quietly dropped aboard us two Moravian missionaries. And it was John who seemed to know just what to do to make the boarding possible. The missionaries recognized him and rewarded him with a smile and thanks, but John appeared unmoved. A moment later he was standing beside me, staring into the torn reflection of the moonlight, held by the same strange affinity that had been working on me.

Early the following morning we cast anchor far within the Inlet, before Rigolet. And as we glided into position, John and I were talking. In his manner was a greater solemnity than ever. I believe now it was the knowledge that in an hour or so his new friend would pass from his life.

"Can you read?" he inquired. And the unusual embarrassment of his manner made me wonder. Then, "Can you write?" And when I modestly admitted both accomplishments he hesitated. I made no effort to draw him out. In a moment he explained. *"I* can, too." There was a great pride in his tone. I recognized it quickly enough to introduce my commendations with the proper spirit. "And I write much," he went on. "I write books."

Having received my cue, I succeeded in finding out that his "books" were diaries written through the winter months of his long season in the interior. For John, the Eskimo, had taught himself to read and write.

"Will you read my books?" he pleaded of me.

We climbed over the side then and sat together in the little boat that was to take us to the Hudson's Bay quay. As I climbed first to the pier a great husky leaped at me. I had heard of huskies and their idiosyncrasies, and I was prepared to put up some fight; but John came tumbling up over the edge and rushed. A sliver of a lad jumped likewise from the other side and drove a kick into the husky's ribs— and then I learned that this particular husky was unwontedly playful. Yet even the Eskimo and the liveyere never trust the husky.

John led me off, past the white buildings of the company, past several ramshackle huts that looked as if a mild wind would make loose lumber of them, and stopped before one a shade more solid than the others, he paused before entering. It was but one of his expressive movements that meant more than words. I was not to follow farther; he did not wish me to see within. I read into it that it was not shame, but a fear that I might not understand his home life. Inside, a few half-hearty words were uttered, and John replied quietly; and presently he appeared with two common exercise books in his hand. These he handed to me and led away from the life of the company buildings and the pier towards an ancient Eskimo burying-ground where we need fear no interruption. It would be a couple of hours before the boat would leave.

But someone shouted. The missionary who had boarded our boat two days before wanted someone to help to unload his household goods, and John, the always ready, supplied the want. And that was the last word I had with him.

I seated myself on the steps of the factor's house and opened one of the books. The first thing I saw was a crude but marvellously lively drawing of a deer. With only a few uncommon lines he had set down a deer in full flight. Therein were none of the rules of drawing, but in his own untrained way John had accomplished what better artists miss. "This is a deer" underneath was but the expression of first principles. And on the second page was a stanza of poetry. Unfortunately it is not at hand, but this dusky son of nature had caught from his mother what he had never read in books. There was meter and rhyme and a strange rhythm, and there was unconscious submission to something working within. I began to read.

It was all about his past winter back there in a frozen world alone. After a time I became suddenly conscious that something was happening beneath me. I started to a cognizance of my surroundings. A husky had crept beneath the step and jerked from beneath me one of a pair of sealskin shoes I had purchased at the store. For huskies are immune from the appeal of an Eskimo's soul. Anything is fodder to the insatiable fire of hunger that burns within.

They were shouting to me from the quay—and there are more attractive dangers than to be marooned on the coast of Labrador. With the diaries I started for the steamer, thinking to meet John there. But on the way we passed his boat returning with its last load. I shouted that I had his books; and his reply was to nod his head slowly, then to rest on his oars a couple of strokes, watching me as we drifted farther apart.

I never saw him again. During the six years that followed I received from him a half-dozen letters a year, all there was time for in the short two months of navigation along the Labrador. I wrote him regularly, sending him such luxuries as I thought would please him and add to his comfort—a camera and supplies, heavy sweater-coats and other comforts, books, writing-paper and pencils, a dictionary. From him there came mementos of his life—a beautiful fox skin for a rug, with head and claws complete; a pair of wooden dolls made entirely by the Eskimo and dressed in exact replica of the sealskin suits of the farthest north; a pair of elk-skin moccasins; a pair of seal gloves. It was significant of John's gallantry that most of these gifts were specifically for the woman-who-worries. For me he was ever on the look for a polar bear skin, and had planned a trip farther north to get one, when other events intervened.

But, best of all, each summer there came out to me his diaries. Diaries have small prospect of breaking through my prejudices, but John's invariably inaugurated a period of seclusion and idleness until

I had read their last word. They were wonderful examples of unstilted, inspired writing. They started with his hunting expedition in the late fall (September, in Labrador) into the interior before the waterways froze over, and through the succeeding eight months, until the threat of breaking ice drove him back to the coast with his furladen sleigh, they recorded his daily life, not as a barren round of uneventfulness, but as a teeming time of throbbing experience. He *felt* everything, from the leap of a running deer to a sunset, from a week's crippling storm to the capture of the much sought silver fox, from the destruction of his tent by fire to the misfortune of pilfering mice. And he had the faculty of making his reader feel with him. In a thumb-nail dash he could take one straight into the clutches of the silent Arctic. Now and then he broke into verse, although in his later diaries this disappeared, perhaps under the goad of more careful register. Breathlessly I would read of the terrible Arctic storms that hemmed him in, all alone in there, hundreds of miles from the nearest human being. And the joys and disappointments of his traps bore almost equally for the moment on the one to whom he was telling his story.

From his diaries I gathered bits of his life. He had left home when only ten years of age, to carve his own fortune, but his father and beloved little sisters were still to him his home, although he never saw them now. He was everyone's friend, grateful for their kindnesses, always ready to help, contemptuous of the lazy Indian, whom he hated. In the summer he fished, or worked for a Grenfell doctor—all mere fill-ups until the hunting season returned. But always there was a note of incomplete existence in his writings, of falling short of his ambitions, of something bigger within the range of his horizon. Even before I waved farewell to him that day, I had him in my mind for a sketch, "John, the Unsatisfied".

Throughout his diaries were many gratifying references to the place I had strangely attained in his affections—communings with himself in the silent nights of the far north. And each summer his letters almost plaintively inquired when I was coming to the Labrador that he might take me away up the Hamilton River to the Grand Falls. Even in his last letter, written from a far distant field, he reintroduced our ancient plans! Once he informed me in his simple way that he had his eye on the liveyere girl for his future home, and asked me to send her a white silk handkerchief with "F" in the corner. John was growing up. During his last summer in Labrador he was much absorbed in an ambition to set up as a Labrador merchant, but he had not the money.

During the first three years of our friendship he embarrassed me much by proposing each summer to come out and visit me; and in one letter he had almost made up his mind to come to me in Canada and take his place permanently in the competition of the white man. I funked the issue each time. I had no fear of his ability to hold his own with brain and hand but the Eskimo in civilization seemed too large a responsibility to assume. At every landing-place in Labrador was, at the time of my visit, a notice threatening a fine of $500 for anyone inducing an Eskimo to leave the country. It was a result of the dire consequences of the Eskimo encampment at the Chicago World's Fair, in 1893. And I could never rid myself of the solemn warning of an Indian chief friend of mine against the risk.

Once a letter arrived in midwinter. The familiar handwriting on the envelope was like a voice from the dead, for I knew Labrador was then frozen in impenetrable ice. Inside I learned that a courier was coming on snow-shoes overland through those hundreds of miles of untracked wastes of Quebec. I replied immediately. And his diary the next summer told of his joy at the receipt in mid-winter of a letter from his friend. A pair of hunters, on their way to their hunting-ground somewhere beyond John, had carried the letter from the little village on the river and left it in one of his tilts.

During the fall of 1914 my letters to him were going astray. His arrived regularly, always lamenting my seeming negligence. A dozen times I wrote on alternate days. The summer of 1915 opened with his diaries and more letters of lonesome plaint. Through June and July they continued. Not a letter of mine was reaching him. Then one day came his despairing effort. On the outside he had written in his most careful hand: "If anyone gets this please send it to Mr. Amy". Whereupon I wrote to St. John's friends to get in touch with John at any cost.

In a couple of his letters he had mentioned his desire to be a soldier, but I had dismissed it as one of his ambitions unattainable owing to his race. In the one that was to be forwarded to me he announced that he had enlisted and was going to England immediately to train.

I ask you to consider that. An Eskimo, a thousand miles from the nearest newspaper—no outside life but that of the Newfoundland fisherman for eight weeks of the year, no industry but hunting and fishing, eight months in the snowbound silences of the most desolate country in the world! And John Shiwak, of another race, untutored, a student only of nature, was going out to fight for his country! Hundreds of thousands of young Canadians could scarcely read it without blushing. Within the little Eskimo was burning that which put conscription beyond the pale.

In the early spring of 1916 I came to England. Within a week I had found where the Newfoundland regiment was in training. John's reply to my letter is too sacred to publish. There was joy in every line of it. "I have nothing to write about," he said as usual, in his simple way. And then he proceeded to impress me with a mission in life I had scarcely appreciated. But he was in Scotland, and I in London. And travel in England is vetoed during the war. Within a very few weeks he was on his way to France, full of ardour.

Almost every week, and sometimes oftener, I heard from him. He was not liking the life. There was something about it he did not understand—this killing of men week after week—and his modesty and reticence, I fear, made him a prey to more assertive fellow soldiers. And thereafter, for months, for some reason, no letter of mine reached him. His petitions for news of me drove me to drastic measures, and then I regained touch with him. Once he was sick in hospital "with his neck", but apart from that he was in the lines every time his battalion was on duty. And after eleven months without leave, suddenly he came to England.

It was unfortunately characteristic of our merely spiritual propinquity that I had left only two days before for a holiday in Devon; and when his wire reached me on a Friday night there was no train to bring him to me and return before Monday night, when he was due in Scotland. I hastened back from Devon to catch him on his way through to France, but the letter he sent me from somewhere in London neglected to include his address, and I could not find him before his train drew out that evening.

His letter of regret, written from Folkestone as he waited for the boat to France, is by me. "I hope we will meet again somewhere," he said, and I imagined a tone of hopelessness rang in it.

Upon his return to France sorrow seemed to dog his steps. He had induced two other Eskimos to enlist with him, but they could not stand the life and were sent back. But his real grief was the loss of his hunting mate, who often shared his winter rounds in Labrador, a white man. "I am the only one left from the Labrador," he moaned. And the longing to get back to his old life peeped from every letter. But to my sympathy and efforts to brighten him he replied: "I am hanging on all right. The only thing to do is to stick it till it's over."

It is through misty eyes I read his letters of those last three months. The duration of the war was wearing on him. He had no close friends, none to keep warm the link with his distant home. In September he lamented: "I have had no letters from home since July. There will be no more now till the ice breaks". And in his last he longed again for the old hunting days. Labrador, that had never satisfied his ambitions, looked warm and friendly to him now. He wondered what the fur would be for the coming winter, what his old friends and people were doing, how the Grenfell doctor managed without him.

I had been sending him books and writing-paper, and small luxuries in food and soldiers' comforts. "It is good to know I have two friends," he thanked me. (The other was a woman living near his training camp in Scotland). "I don't think a man could be better off." Simple, grateful John! He complained of the cold, and I despatched a warm sweater and a pair of woollen gloves. But they never reached him.

That was in mid-November. A month later an official envelope came to me. Inside was my last letter. On its face was the soulless stamp. "Deceased". More sympathetic hands had added: "Killed", "Verified".

It was a damp-eyed sergeant told me of his end, this native of Labrador, the only Eskimo to lay down his life for the Empire.

"He was a white man," he whispered. Would that John could have heard it! It happened in the Cambrai tank drive. The tanks were held up by the canal before Masnieres, and John's company was ordered to rush a narrow bridge that had unaccountably been left standing. John, chief sniper of his battalion, lately promoted lance-corporal, the muscular son of the wilds, outpaced his comrades. The battalion still discusses which was the first to reach the bridge, John or another. But John ran to the height of the little arch and turned to wave his companions on.

It was a deadly corner of the battlefield. The Germans, granted a respite by the obstacle of the canal, were rallying. Big shells were dropping everywhere, scores of machine guns were beginning to bark across the narrow line of protecting water. And just beyond the bridge-head, in among the trees, the enemy had erected a platform in tiers, bearing machine guns. As John stood, his helmet awry, his mouth open in unheard shouts of encouragement, the deadly group of machine guns broke loose. That was why the bridge had been left.

The Eskimo swayed, then sank slowly. But even as he lay they saw his hand point ahead. And then he lay still. And they passed him on the bridge, lying straight and peaceful, gone to a better hunting-ground than he had ever known.

And my thoughts of John Shiwak, the Eskimo, to-day, are that he must have been satisfied at the last.

A fisherman's family in Labrador. They are seen wearing their best clothes. John Shiwak, our hero, in a new suit which he bought at St. John's, Newfoundland, is the figure on the extreme right. The fisherman's home is an old boat.